Irving
Berlin

Fingers on the black notes (*National Film Archive*)

Irving Berlin

MICHAEL FREEDLAND

STEIN AND DAY/Publishers/New York

62061

First published in 1974

Copyright © 1974 by Michael Freedland

Library of Congress Catalog Card No. 73–90699

All rights reserved

Designed by David Miller

Printed in the United States of America

Stein and Day/*Publishers*/Scarborough House, Briarcliff Manor, N.Y. 10510

ISBN 0–8128–1659–5

For my children
FIONA, DANI, and JONATHAN
who had the good sense to
choose my wife as their mother

Contents

Acknowledgments

IRVING BERLIN WILL always be, for me, the world's greatest weaver of musical spells. When I did a radio program about him for the BBC it was the fulfillment of a long-standing ambition. Talking to him was an experience never to be forgotten, something to tell one's grandchildren. So to Irving Berlin must go my first thanks, although he never wanted a book written about him.

This is above all a show business story, so thanks also to the giants of the entertainment world, the performers and the music people who helped me flesh out the tale by granting me interviews: Bing Crosby, Fred Astaire, Ethel Merman, Johnny Mercer, Irving Caesar, Walter Scharf, Morris Stoloff. The late Abel Green of *Variety*, a paper justly called the Bible of show business, was a tremendous help with source material. To Ginette Spanier, special thanks for recounting a very personal interlude; my gratitude also to numerous people who, for reasons I respect, would not like to have their names published.

I thank Beryl Whiteman and Merle Booth for their help in typing the manuscript, and the captain of the typing team, my wife, who had to tolerate so much for so long.

My thanks end where they began, to Irving Berlin, who has given so much to so many.

MICHAEL FREEDLAND

1

Say It with Music

IN THE SMITHSONIAN Institution in Washington, D.C., stands an old upright piano whose mahogany woodwork bears distinct signs of wear. The keys are yellowed; it is obvious that some of them have been used over the years more for balancing cigarettes than for making music.

A similar piano, bearing the marks of similar wear, stands in an office in Manhattan. Two things about both of them set them apart from other pianos. One is a lever underneath the keyboard that can change the sound of the notes struck, just as the movement of a gearshift in a car can change the sound of the engine. The other thing they have in common is that they are both instruments on which Irving Berlin transformed the popular song.

In all his years (he was born in 1888), Irving Berlin never learned how to play a conventional piano properly. He created something like 3,000 songs and influenced practically every songwriter for three generations by pounding the black notes in the key of F sharp and by using that little lever to convert them into a fuller range of sound. He has never learned how to read music.

Three thousand songs? Only about half of them have been published, a number in itself a world record. Berlin himself told me, "A song becomes a hit and sells perhaps 7,500 copies. To the

11

songwriter it's always two million. But the figures for 'White Christmas,' they are really very impressive—up to seventy million."

And that's Berlin himself—very impressive. A small man, five feet five inches tall. Very intense. Very jealous of his reputation. Very shy about himself. But very impressive. And deservedly admired as no other songwriter has ever been, either by his contemporaries or by people like me, who still cherish the memory of being a little boy sitting in a theater gallery and listening to a song called "This Is the Army, Mr. Jones."

Fred Astaire told me, "Irving Berlin was the first honest-to-goodness melody writer I can remember. He started the whole thing."

Jerome Kern said, "Irving Berlin has no place in American music. He *is* American music."

In reply to such tributes, the husky Berlin voice feigns modesty. "My average for hits is pretty good. I'll say that. But I've probably written more flops than anyone else, too."

He says there is no recipe for successful songwriting. "More people can write a catchy tune than good verses." He himself has been writing both for almost seventy years, love songs, patriotic songs, ragtime, blues, comedy songs, and pop songs.

"Berlin has an institutional monicker," said Harold Arlen. He meant that Irving Berlin has been both the Ford and the General Motors of the American song industry. Twenty Broadway shows and seventeen Hollywood musicals testify to that.

But he was reluctant to allow his story to be told. "I'll give you a few headlines," he told me. "But no real story—yet."

It is a story crying out to be told, as though a character in a Berlin musical were waiting in the wings ready to go into the big number—Berlin himself.

Jerome Kern summed it up, "When at last the composer of The Great American Opera sets out to find a libretto he might look further but fare worse than Berlin's own story."

The real pity is that those two worn pianos cannot talk as well as they have been made to sing. So this is what could not have come from a musical keyboard, the story of a composer who always calls himself a songwriter, whose timeless songs to him are no more than "tunes."

The Irving Berlin story on the white keys as well as the black.

2

Give Me Your Tired, Your Poor

THE SIGHT OF A blazing house and the comforting feel of a feather-bed quilt are the two abiding memories Irving Berlin has of Temun. Temun was in Siberia, and it was there that Moses Baline and his wife Leah had their home and where their eight children were born.

Israel was four years old and small for his age. He had big black eyes and a shock of black hair. On the day of the fire he clung to his mother's arms while she pulled him close and hugged him in a quilt. With Moses and the other children they stood in a field and watched the fire rage. It is easy to imagine Moses Baline, a cantor in the local synagogue, murmuring a prayer in Hebrew.

The Cossacks had declared a pogrom and Temun's Jews knew what to expect. Moses and Leah bundled the children and their few belongings together, knowing that their only chance was to get away before they were found. With their tiny home in smoldering ruins, Moses was only too grateful that God had chosen to spare his family.

Jews had wandered to Siberia, that far-off corner of Russia, in the same way that others had gone to Lithuania and Poland. "We weren't all political prisoners there, you know," Berlin is fond of saying now.

It was in Siberia that Moses Baline and Leah Lipkin had first met, but now the Baline couple had no choice but to try to join

14

their cousin in America. Scores of other families in the neighborhood had done so already, and, by all accounts, the streets of New York were paved with gold. It was 1892.

The Baline family followed the familiar trek of other Russian Jews driven from Siberia, through to the Jewish Pale of Settlement, then on to Latvia, Lithuania, the Baltic coast, and the long journey to a promised land.

On the boat for the painful month-long voyage, the Balines and their fellow passengers were herded together like a mass of human cattle, but at least there was a new life to look forward to. At the sight of the Statue of Liberty, their hearts rose. Emma Lazarus had written, "Give me your tired, your poor . . ." and a generation later a new composer would create a song called "God Bless America." The immigrants learned that this wasn't really America yet. They had landed on Ellis Island, a kind of no-man's land in the shadow of Manhattan. All personal particulars had to be noted. Little cards were made out and stored away. The fact that Israel Baline had been allowed into America was cross-indexed and registered for posterity in a filing cabinet.

Strange voices in strange accents shouted above the sound of the steam funnels. The clatter of horses' hooves on the cobblestones made a noise that was frightening for children as young as Israel. The Balines chatted to each other in Yiddish while gathering their packages, a pitifully small bundle of treasures, around them. Being in a new country is hard, but the Balines at least had a guide to show them America.

Moses's cousin had been bright enough to emigrate to the United States some years before, and had written back to Temun of the wonderful things in America, so he was the family celebrity. They had talked of him in hushed, respectful tones.

On this day, the respect began to dwindle. Their cousin did not seem quite so prosperous as they had thought he would be. Certainly he was dressed like an American. No more for him the long coat and the wide-brimmed hat which in Europe had seemed to a Jew as much a part of him as his beard.

But it was not just a question of the cousin's appearance. As the horse-drawn buggy took them through New York, through the Battery and the Bowery, it was clear there was no gold paving these streets. The buildings were as high as they had been described in letters. But they were not like temples or palaces, no onion domes reaching to the sky. Just one shapeless building after another, dirty black buildings with an occasional fire escape to relieve the monotony.

Finally the Balines and their escort arrived on the lower East Side, where so many other immigrants had come before. The East Side was already a melting pot of Italy, Germany, Ireland, and Jewish Russia. The apartment their cousin had arranged for them was on Monroe Street. There were no windows in any of the three tiny rooms which they had been allocated. There was only filth and noise from passing traffic, noise from children crying in adjoining rooms.

The first place Moses went after settling his family was to the nearest synagogue. Perhaps they could offer him a job?

But New York hardly needed cantors. They had streamed off every boat. Moses eventually found a job as a *shomer*, a supervisor in a kosher slaughterhouse. In the Jewish community's eyes, religious functionaries came no lower, but Moses was grateful for the work. He watched over meats the like of which he could never afford to bring to his own table, meat for families who had managed to move out of Monroe Street. And that made him determined to bring his family out of the squalor of their new home as quickly as possible.

The children of other new arrivals, youngsters like his Izzy, were just beginning to speak English; some had already been entered in the local public schools. But all had parents who wanted them to retain some of the religion that they had brought over with them. Out of what little money any of these parents earned, they put by a few cents for the *malamud*, the teacher who gave Hebrew lessons. So Moses became a *malamud*, going to work at the slaughterhouse early in the morning so that he could come home with time still left to visit his students, young boys who were being forcibly prevented from joining their new neighbors in games of baseball so that they could be steeped in the wisdom he offered. Even on the Sabbath he worked to earn a few cents more. The synagogue had its own cantor, but there were times when a deputy was needed, when someone had to help train the choir. Those jobs Moses took on as well. Young Izzy liked nothing more than to be able to join his father by singing in the choir. Before very long Moses had made just enough to move out of the squalor of Monroe Street and travel a few blocks with the family's belongings to a slightly better apartment on Cherry Street.

At seven, Izzy was sent to the local public school. His teachers reported to his parents that they found him very lazy. "He just dreams and sings to himself," one teacher commented. He was much more excited by the color of the polyglot neighborhood: Italians, Chinese, Poles. He soaked up the songs he heard on the streets, Yiddish, Italian, it made no difference to the boy who sang them. And, of course, far better than school was going to the synagogue with his father. "I suppose it was singing with my father that gave me my musical background," he recalled later. "It was in my blood." Pleasures were few but they came cheap. When he was not singing, and he could get away from the four walls at home and at school, he would go swimming in the East River, just a stone's throw from Cherry Street.

Years later he said, "There were eight or nine of us living in four rooms, and in summer some of us slept on the fire escape or on the roof. I was a boy with poor parents, but I didn't starve. I was never hungry. There was always bread and butter and hot tea."

In 1896 Moses Baline died. Izzy was eight years old when he saw his father's rough wood coffin carried off to the cemetery. He made up his mind then that he was going to help his mother by leaving school to earn a living. So in the second grade, he packed up his books for the last time and said goodbye to the kids who had sat in the desks next to his. He was going to sell newspapers. A friend told him that the distributors of the *New York Evening Journal* wanted young sellers.

Mother Baline had a ritual for collecting the money her children earned, Izzy and the older children who already had jobs. In the evening, she would sit in her hard wooden chair, holding out her apron. Into it the children dropped the coins they had amassed during the day. On the day Izzy joined the city's business population there was no happier face in all New York. He followed his brothers and sisters as they queued up to drop money in Leah's apron, and there was a coin from him, too. Three coins, in fact, the three cents he had made that day.

Selling papers and bringing the proceeds home with him gave young Izzy a sense of independence he had never known. When he walked back to Cherry Street along the banks of the East River he felt joyous about the money jingling in his pockets.

One day, walking along the dockside, he was mesmerized by a ship unloading before him, a British boat bound for China. He was so intoxicated by the excitement before him that he didn't notice the giant boom of a crane rushing toward him. The ship's crew shouted, but not in time. The crane knocked the little boy off his feet and carried him out into the oily black river. He was lucky. Within moments an Irish seaman had jumped off the ship and had young Izzy by the scruff of the neck. Quickly he passed him to another man who had raced to the edge of the dock.

Wringing wet, water gushing from his mouth and out of his shirt and trousers, Izzy was hauled ashore. Taken on board, the boy was rubbed down with towels and given a hot drink. "I was scared," he said years afterward. "More scared than at any time till the Wall Street crash."

The sailors who had been so kind to this boy with the curly black hair and big eyes were unable to pry open his right hand. Throughout the episode, Izzy had managed to clutch the four cents he had made for himself that day. Dried off, he walked home and deposited coins in his mother's lap as usual.

Selling the *Evening Journal* introduced Izzy to a completely new kind of people, not at all the sort his father would have wanted to know. Many of them worked in the beer halls and the flophouses of the Bowery. One evening he followed them to one of the saloons. The noise was deafening. The smoke almost overpowering. But it attracted him as nothing else ever had before. He waited by the swinging latticed half-doors, not daring to go in. When the doors opened he saw waiters passing the foaming glasses of beer over the heads of the patrons. The men in the long white aprons carried the glasses on trays which they managed to balance on one hand.

Sometimes, when they were not serving, the waiters would group together and, with a cloth over one arm and the other arm free to twirl a waxed moustache, they would sing as they passed among the patrons, collecting coins thrown in their trays.

The sight and sound of all this left Izzy spellbound. After listening to a song two or three times he would stand on a street corner and sing the same ballad to passersby. The result was exactly what he had hoped for. The people threw pennies at him.

These were the riches of dreams. Newspapers to sell in the afternoon, songs to sing for money in the evening. But what if he were to sing *inside* the saloons?

He went home that night, deposited the new fortune in his mother's lap and announced: "Ma, I want to work as a singing waiter."

It was as though he had said he wanted to become a pimp. Leah was shocked to think that her son, the offspring of a man who had sung in the synagogue, could contemplate such heathen thoughts.

"I'll buy you a new rocking chair one day, Ma," he told her.

From her reaction, Izzy felt that there was only one way he could do it, namely by running away.

That first night away, he huddled in a tenement lobby. The next day, he went the rounds of the saloons, offering his services. He was not in the sort of demand he expected to be. No one had a job for him but Blind Sol who went the rounds of the Bowery haunts singing the lachrymose ballads of the period. It was difficult for Sol to get from place to place, so he and young Izzy arranged that Izzy would accompany him for a small percentage of the old man's takings. At the end of the first day, Izzy had made fifteen cents, enough for a night under the roof of a cheap hotel.

After a few weeks of helping the blind singer, however, Izzy moved on. After all, he wanted to do the singing himself. Occasionally, he got a one-night job inside a tavern. Other times, there was nothing for him, and so there was nowhere to sleep. Cold, or soaked to the skin, he would take refuge in the basement of a neighborhood shop or bar. When his shirt got too dirty for even a fourteen-year-old to tolerate, he would wash it in a street fountain and then creep into the boiler room of a big building to dry it near a furnace.

Despondent, he stuck to it, and then the Bowery's word of mouth worked for him. Someone had heard him sing the George M. Cohan songs he loved, tunes like "Mary's a Grand Old Name" and "Give My Regards to Broadway," and he was invited to come to the offices of music publisher Harry von Tilzer.

In those pre-radio days, records were novelties for the rich, and the music business thrived on the sheet music of tunes that customers bought to play and sing around their parlor pianos. The only way the public could get to know whether or not a song was what they wanted was by hearing it. So song pluggers worked for different music publishers, cramming the booths of music shops to play and sing the songs to customers.

Publishers also paid entertainers to sing their songs from the stage. Von Tilzer was going one better than that. After one of *his* singers had finished a song, by some spontaneous magic a member of the audience would get up and sing the same song, knowing the words as though he had been given a sheet of the music and lyrics to study. Before long, there was a spotlight on this talented "customer," and with the rest of the audience humming in accompaniment, he would sing his heart out.

Von Tilzer took Izzy on as a talented member of the audience to "cover" artists on the bill. Izzy was elated to discover that he'd be performing this task (for five dollars a week!) at Tony Pastor's famous Music Hall at Union Square.

Tony Pastor's. Everyone in vaudeville looked enviously at contemporaries given the chance to play there. Izzy did not know at the time that this was the very theater where the kind of number that was to have a considerable influence on his kind of music had had its debut. A few years before, Ben Harvey had played his "Piano Rag" on the stage there, and the popular song never quite seemed the same again.

Von Tilzer paid Izzy his money and Izzy sang his tunes as well as others by another Tin Pan Alley character, Paul Dresser. It was a happy time. Izzy was being introduced to the people of show business. Among these was a family trio whose act he followed, The Three Keatons, Mom and Dad Keaton and their sad-eyed little boy everyone knew as Buster. A few years later that youngster became a cult hero of the silent screen.

Like all good things, however, the stint at Tony Pastor's came to an end. Izzy went back to catching irregular opportunities at different Bowery night spots. If he was lucky, he earned fifteen cents, just enough to put up in a cheap boardinghouse. At Callaghan's, one of the most famous of the dives, he was rewarded not just with pennies but with a chance to stay the night. He was also given the dignity of being asked to sign the register.

Among his new-found friends in the business of singing was a youngster called George White, who was soon to electrify Broadway with his famous "Scandals" revues.

Finally this sixteen-year-old veteran of show business was offered a permanent job by a man known as "Nigger" Mike Salter who ran a beer hall in Chinatown.

3

I Love a Piano

"NIGGER" MIKE WAS A man of his times and so was his "Pelham's Cafe." Both were misnomers. Salter was a white man, but so swarthy that his clientele thought he justified the nickname. As for his cafe, it was as much a brothel as an eating place.

The real attractions of Pelham's were the beer it dispensed and the big-bosomed girls who, for the mere encouragement of a wink, would drape themselves around the customers, revealing a new inch of flesh for every extra dime they were offered.

The charms of the girls and the smoke-engulfed wooden tables attracted sailors, occasional college students, and ward heelers who used it as a center for settling their differences. And the Chinese population gathered there to extend the Tong feuds they had brought with them from the old country. Often there was as much blood to be washed from the floor as there was beer to be mopped up.

Izzy, who had been reconciled with Leah, reported for work at eight every night and was on duty until six the next morning, "slinging out plates of hash and serving beers," as he described it. A glass of beer was five cents, whiskey was ten cents. Izzy's other services were officially free.

With the tray in his left hand and the serving cloth over his right arm, he would break into song. If the customers liked it, they clapped and made his tray rattle with coins. If they didn't, it was the one time the place was ever quiet.

Izzy learned how to judge his customers. He knew which were going to throw coins even if they didn't care that much for his song, and which would have been ungenerous even toward Enrico Caruso. Every time a coin rattled in the tray above him—and because of his height he had to stretch higher than most of his colleagues—he imagined a new rocking chair for his mother that much more vividly.

One of the most popular attractions at Pelham's was an apartment above the cafe reserved for a well-known madam called Chinatown Gertie. Parties of tourists, slumming for the evening, would be taken there as a high spot of their trip. A man with a megaphone would lead them. As Gertie opened her door, he would hand her a dollar bill. It was a signal for the rest of the party to do the same. After the visitors had left, the man with the megaphone returned and split the tourist takings with Gertie.

One of the bleary-eyed Pelham's regulars was "Hobnailed Casey." He sat at the same table every night with a glass of beer in front of him and did little but stare around him and clean his fingernails. It was a good excuse to keep his penknife constantly open. One night though, when Casey's penknife was not at the ready, a man called Frisco Joe murdered him in the middle of the crowded cafe. Izzy was expected to go on singing just as though Casey were still there, still cleaning his fingernails. And he did, all the familiar Cohan ballads, "Push Me Along in My Pushcart," "Ring to the Name of Rosie," and a new favorite, "Yankee Doodle Boy." After all, Izzy was now being paid seven dollars a week for professional services.

On another night there was a group of visitors who accompanied a jovial, bearded gentleman with a slight German accent.

Mike recognized him instantly. "It's the Prince," he told his bartender, Sulky. "The Prince who's in the papers." Indeed, for days, New York's papers had been full of stories about the arrival of Prince Louis of Battenberg, the German-born cousin of the man who would soon be England's King George V, who had become one of the senior officers of the Royal Navy.

It was a popular sport in those days for important visitors from abroad to be shown the seamier side of New York life. Mike deferentially conducted the Prince to a table. Would the Prince like some beer? The Prince would indeed. Mike snapped his fingers and the nearest waiter was instantly there. And would the Prince like a song? Of course. So the waiter who had brought the drinks began nervously to warble. Izzy Baline singing to royalty! "Wait till I tell Ma," he thought as the Prince clapped, then moistened his beard with more beer.

When the group left, Mike was at the door to say goodbye, to note how much he appreciated the royal patronage, and to hope the Prince would find it possible to come again. Prince Louis, in turn, displayed his appreciation of such kind thoughts, and from his wallet pulled a cluster of bills to offer Mike. "No sir," was the reply. "It was payment enough to have the honor of your presence." Instead of putting the money back in his wallet, the Prince turned to the young waiter who had entertained him. "For you, young man," he said.

"No sir," gulped the dark-eyed seventeen-year-old. "It was my honor to sing." Only later he thought of how many weeks' worth of tips he had blown in being carried away by the occasion.

The Prince's party had not consisted solely of aides. There were reporters among them too, the same newspapermen who had faithfully recorded the Prince's arrival and his more official engagements at City Hall, in Wall Street, at the New York Naval detachment. Tonight they had a more human story to tell, and in the *New York World* a young reporter named Herbert Bayard Swope gave Baline his first press notice.

Izzy had by now made a discovery that truly excited him. By pounding the black notes on the old upright piano used by Mike's resident musician, Nick Nicholson, Izzy could make tunes himself, halting, but recognizable. Then he began thinking about making up his own tunes. Years later he said, "Once you start singing, you start thinking of writing your own songs. It's as simple as that."

Morning after morning, as soon as the customers had all gone and the floor was swept and the tables sponged and the chairs stacked, he would race to that old upright. He toyed with all the tunes he knew. Those he was singing nightly at Pelham's, those he had sung from the balcony of Tony Pastor's, and those that had earned him pennies on Bowery corners. Nick Nicholson kept his music under the piano stool, but learning music in its printed form was never what interested Izzy.

Leah Baline, who, thanks to her son's savings, would before long have a gleaming new mahogany rocking chair, accepted Izzy's ambitions without being able to understand them. She admired the long hours he worked and was secretly impressed by his news that he could pound the black keys of a piano and produce sounds recognizable as "music."

Callaghan's, a rival saloon in Chinatown, had a pianist, Al Piantadosi, who was slowly making a name for himself by having written an Italian dialect song called "My Muriuccia Take a Steamboat." In an age when immigrants were nostalgic about their home countries and native-born Americans joked about the newcomers, a song like "My Muriuccia" quickly became a hit. And it meant good publicity for Callaghan's.

Mike was furious. "We gotta have a song of our own," he demanded of his waiters as soon as he realized the impact of "My Muriuccia." Izzy accepted the challenge. He talked to Nick Nicholson and between them, Nick supplying the music, Izzy the words, they came up with "Marie from Sunny Italy."

The night that Izzy scribbled the words on his celluloid cuffs he sang them for the assembled customers at Pelham's. A couple of days later the song was in print. He was, of course, unable to read the notes that went with his lyrics. But the sheet music made history because of a printer's error. The name printed on the cover read: I. Berlin.

Izzy liked the printer's mistake. Berlin, he thought, had a touch of class to it. He also liked the idea of making money by writing songs, but that didn't come quite as easily as the instant satisfaction of seeing his new name in print. The tune earned a grand total of seventy-five cents in royalties which, by the time Nick Nicholson had had his share, meant that Mr. Berlin was worth thirty-seven cents more than he had been before. It had been agreed that the odd penny should go to Mr. Nicholson.

With his mother's chair now bought, Izzy was saving enough from his seven dollars a week plus tips to buy himself something. A traveling salesman who called at the saloon one evening sold him a small diamond ring without giving too many details about how it had been acquired.

These were times when the pressures under which the youngster was working were so great that he often fell asleep in the back of the saloon. One such evening another waiter removed the ring from Izzy's finger as he slept, while a second man took all the money from the cafe's till. It was meant as a prank. Mike did not think much of the joke. Izzy was out on his neck.

His next singing-waitership was in Union Square, in a bar owned by one-time boxing champion Jimmy Kelly. Socially, Kelly's was a step up from Pelham's. Berlin sang more Cohan songs and worked on something new of his own, parodying original verses to match tunes. He didn't try to be too scrupulous about rhyme. He could follow "queen" with "mandolin" and "patiently" with "happy be" and feel quite satisfied. And he went on experimenting with songs of his own. Early in 1908, he hummed a few bars of music which he thought went well with a lyric called "The Best of Friends Must Part." The pianist at Kelly's played it over for him and wrote down the notes. Izzy seemed content enough with that way of getting a melody down on paper.

With another friend, he wrote a song called "Queenie My Own," a song he sold and actually heard other people sing. In the long run "Queenie" flopped, but not before Izzy had turned out another lyric called "She Was a Dear Little Girl." That was bought by Marie Cahill, a popular stage singer who featured it in her show *The Boys and Betty*.

Izzy was happy if not rich. But then a story hit the newspapers that changed both his life and that of the popular music scene. An Italian waiter named Dorando appeared to win the Marathon race at the 1908 London Olympic Games only to be disqualified when frenzied spectators rushed toward him and pushed the athlete inches toward the finishing tape. The judges decided he had broken the rules by being "helped" to victory, and an American named Hayes was declared the winner.

The poor Italian's disaster at the hands of well-meaning spectators was an event that fired saloon conversation for weeks. In the wake of its actual happening, however, young Berlin served beer to a vaudeville song-and-dance man who was always on the lookout for material he could buy cheap. At Kelly's that night, he told his waiter he wanted a song in Italian dialect which he could use between two more sober numbers. He was willing to pay ten dollars.

Shades of "Marie from Sunny Italy." To Berlin it was a perfect challenge. The name Dorando was on everyone's lips. But how do you write a comedy song about a man's loss? You make it about a man who had *bet* on the loser, that's how! Izzy's lyrics would be about another Italian, a barber who had put his whole fortune on the runner.

When the vaudevillian came into Kelly's again, Berlin and his verses were ready. But the entertainer had changed his mind. What he really needed was a new dance routine. He certainly wasn't going to pay ten dollars for a song.

Berlin decided it was time to present himself to Tin Pan Alley. Ted Snyder, a well-known music publisher, had his office there. Israel Baline was met by Henry Waterson, Snyder's general manager. "My name is Irving Berlin," the youngster said. He had planned this moment. "Israel" had too Biblical a sound for a songwriter, he had decided, and "Izzy" certainly didn't sound right. "Irving," on the other hand, had a nice lilt to it. "You have music to go with these words?" Waterson asked Berlin. "Of course," the newly renamed Irving lied, and followed the manager into the back room. There he was introduced to a man at a piano. "Hum it to him and he'll play it for you," Waterson advised. In that moment, one of the techniques that Berlin followed for more than sixty years was firmly established.

Now he was in a spot that required not only all the talent he could muster, but also all the nerve. Somehow, he improvised a tune, the pianist set down the notes, and "Dorando" was presented as a package, first to Waterson and then to Snyder himself.

"We'll publish it," Snyder promised, and then astonished Berlin with a real job offer. "Come work for me. I'll give you $25 a week as a staff composer."

The first person to be told, of course, was his mother. There was a lot more money than usual to be poured into the old lady's apron that night.

4

Alexander's Ragtime Band

SNYDER TOOK BERLIN UNDER his wing and asked him to write more lyrics for which the publisher himself would supply the tunes. The verses were not very distinguished at first. "Christmas Time Seems Years and Years Away" (he'd do better with that theme a couple of generations later) and "Do Your Duty, Doctor" were two of them. But there were also more sophisticated Snyder-Berlin ballads, like "I Didn't Go Home at All" and "I Wish That You Was My Gal, Molly."

It was easy to see where Berlin's influence lay: in the wings of the theatre where George M. Cohan's numbers rocked the audiences and had them cheering the sight of the American flag as it was draped along the boards. (Cohan was once asked if he could write a show without a flag in it and he replied, "I can write without anything but a pencil.") Berlin still remembers Cohan as "my inspiration, the model, the idol. We all start as imitators of somebody." But he adds, "If you continue to imitate, then you're not a songwriter. Once you express your own talent, it's a question of how good you are."

Berlin was good enough to earn four thousand dollars in royalties from "Dorando." Everything he wrote, he enjoyed. Snyder supplied most of the tunes, but occasionally Irving worked with other composers. Al Piantadosi, the man from Callaghan's who wrote "My Muriuccia Take a Steamboat," and he came up with a romantic piece of nonsense called "Just Like the Rose."

In the same year, 1909, a Berlin-Snyder song was heard on Coney Island at Carey Walsh's Saloon. There, a youngster who was still a singing waiter used it to collect coins in his own tray while he still dreamed of doing better things himself. His name was Eddie Cantor.

Snyder was proud of his new wordsmith and introduced him to other musicians, among them, a man named Edgar Leslie. He and Irving dreamed up a number intended as a put-down of the Eastern mystique that had women swooning and men climbing walls. The song was called "Sadie Salome—Go Home."

The song was an admitted parody of another, but the public loved it. Three hundred thousand copies were sold. "As much as anything," Berlin said years later, "we did it to see whether we could get away with it." Parody of his own music is something he's never allowed anyone else to get away with. He has frequently taken legal action against those who tried. Yet in 1909 he came up with "That Mesmerizing Mendelssohn Tune," which he based on the classic "Spring Song," and the dollars rolled in as sales reached five hundred thousand copies.

To explain having done what he would never have accepted of another doing to his work, he said, "I had always loved Mendelssohn and his 'Spring Song' and simply wanted to work it into a rag tune."

He was taking his inspiration now from anywhere he found it. The chance word of a passerby, someone's brief whistling, a glimpse of skyline—all bred lyrics.

Berlin was now, at twenty-one, a dapper young fellow with his own apartment and fine clothes: stiff collar, smart waistcoated suit, spats over impeccably polished shoes.

It was while having them shined at a barbershop off Tin Pan Alley that another song was conceived. A friend named George Whiting, also in the barbershop, and also in the songwriting business, suggested they go to a theatre that night. He was free, he explained, "My wife's gone to the country."

"Hooray," shouted Berlin. And then, with mouth agape, he thought about what he had said.

"We're *not* going to the theater tonight," he told Whiting. "We've got ourselves a song."

They called in Snyder to help with the melody and the song became "My Wife's Gone to the Country—Hoorah! Hoorah!"

For Berlin the song was merely a case of instant inspiration. Whiting must have had mixed feelings, for as a result of this collaboration, his wife not only went to the country—she left him for good. There are no reports that he shouted "Hoorah!" after their divorce became final. But it is on record that he had second thoughts eventually about the institution of marriage, with a song called "My Blue Heaven."

If Whiting had been unhappy about his wife's leaving him, he certainly couldn't have grumbled about the money to which that fatal "Hoorah!" led. Three hundred thousand copies of the tune were sold.

Now Irving's mother, accompanied by his brothers and sisters, could move to a bigger apartment, aglow in the glory of "My son, the songwriter."

And the glory that was Irving Berlin then was reflected not only from the pages of sheet music, but from the pages of the *New York Journal*, which paid him generously to write a hundred new verses for "My Wife's Gone to the Country." All the lyrics, and he must shudder at the memory now, were parodies of what he and Whiting had originally produced.

Soon, for the first time, Irving went behind the footlights of a theatre in which the audience did not smell of beer. The chairs were padded and the floor was carpeted, and he heard himself introduced to one of the legendary names of Broadway, Jake Shubert.

It is difficult to think of Broadway impresarios more successful or influential or hated than Jake and his brother Lee. Between them, before long, they cornered the market on Broadway theaters, owning more than half of them, as well as most of the big playhouses in the other towns and cities of the country. They were hated by other people in the business because of the way they rode over their own performers as well as over competitors. They also hated each other. Every triumph for Jake led to a crusade by Lee to better his brother's achievement.

No one could deny that they were shrewd—shrewd enough to recognize the potential of a young blackface singer called Al Jolson when he appeared in a minor spot on the opening night of their new theater, the Winter Garden. Two years later they had made Al Jolson a star. But they also made Irving Berlin more than just a songwriter. He became an entertainer. In *Up and Down Broadway,* in 1910, he was feted as a man who had made it big singing all his own songs. A big success.

So successful that the Columbia Record Company signed him to record his songs. He started with "Oh, How That German Could Love." And that was the end of it. Neither the high Berlin voice nor the Berlin piano did justice to his songs. It may be sad, now, to reflect on what posterity has missed, but his voice, on records, was only mildly pleasant. He was no Jolson.

It was clear, however, that Irving Berlin, songwriter, liked being in the public eye. Despite being shy, he enjoyed having a public. The exposure of being seen and being talked about helped to spell success at music shop cash registers.

One of the tunes that Berlin, with Ted Snyder accompanying him on the piano, produced for *Up and Down Broadway* was "That Beautiful Rag." It was more than a prophetic title. For this was the dawning of the ragtime age in American popular music. There had been "rags" since the last days of the nineteenth century. But few of them had yet produced riches. Irving Berlin was out to change all that, by adopting as his own the jazz form that became grandfather to all modern pop varieties, right up to rock and roll.

Berlin and Snyder now produced "That Opera Rag" and a ditty called "Alexander and His Clarinet." Jack Alexander was a young bandleader who was cutting quite a swath among the jazz crowd in those years. To Berlin, a man who could find inspiration for a song in a friend's wife going to the country, there was no reason not to model a lyric on the name of a real musician. Nothing very much happened with "Alexander and His Clarinet." But add a whole band to that clarinet, Irving was convinced, and it would be an entirely different matter.

A year before, Berlin had decided he did not always want to be dependent on people like Ted Snyder to produce his music for him. The urge to play out his own melodies was getting stronger. He still could not play the piano properly, but he could fashion a melody by moving his fingers, hesitantly, over the black keys of F sharp. What he could not do was make the white keys sound effective. This was 1909, though, and he thought modern science might have begun to devise solutions to problems like the one he posed. (What he did not realize was that at least a century earlier, the firm of Norris and Hyde in London had first produced a piano that could change keys for the pianist.)

He made inquiries and found that the Weser Company in the United States could make what he needed. All he would have to do was adjust a lever under the keyboard. It cost him a hundred dollars. But it made the poor boy from Russia feel like Tchaikovsky. It also helped turn him into a national institution. He began thumping out something he called "Alexander's Ragtime Band."

When it sounded roughly the way he wanted it to, he called in one of Snyder's arrangers and played the piece to him. With that gesture, in 1910, a tune made history. Nothing less could be said of a piece of music that altered the entire course of the popular song.

"Ragtime was written years before I ever thought of a phrase," Berlin says now. "But what I did was crystallize it. Music is music, and there are only two kinds that I know of," he adds. "Good music and bad."

There were no words for "Alexander" at first. Berlin did not think he needed any. But his colleagues at Snyder's did not fancy publishing it, so Berlin shelved it for the time being. It stayed in his thoughts, though it was the one number he couldn't sell. He began pinning his hopes on a new contact.

Jesse Lasky, a new force on Broadway, had not yet thought of extending his empire across the country to Hollywood, and his sister had not yet married Samuel Goldwyn. But he had opened Broadway's first big restaurant-cum-theater and expected great things from it. His place was called The Folies Bérgère, more than a little modeled on its French namesake and, Lasky hoped, destined for the same kind of unfading success.

For his opening show, Lasky had brought over from London "the Hebraicly-beautiful" star of England's music halls, Ethel Levey. He asked Berlin to provide a new song for his sensational import. Berlin did. With Ted Snyder again furnishing the tune, it was called "I Beg Your Pardon, Dear Old Broadway."

Lasky liked it and bought another Berlin-Snyder song to go with it, a tune called "Spanish Love." Now came the sales pitch. Lasky seemed to be in the mood for still another new number, and Berlin just happened to have one up his sleeve.

"I'll play it for you myself," he said, and did. Lasky just sat and nodded.

"Play it again, Irving," the showman requested. And doing the best he could without the aid of a levered piano, Berlin played it again.

"You like it?" he asked Lasky.

"There's something in it. Play it again."

And again he played it, feeling that much more confident now.

"You think it's good?"

"Well," said Lasky, slowly and seriously. "I wouldn't go as far as to say that. But I might be able to use it."

The lyricless "Alexander's Ragtime Band" had its first public performance by an orchestra on the opening night of the Folies Bérgère's *International Revue*. But it appeared that the audience was much more interested in the decor, the girls, the champagne, and the menu than they were in the music.

Later in the evening, the tune had a second performance when

Otis Harlan came out and whistled it. Harlan many years later achieved a modest anonymous success as the voice of "Happy," one of the Dwarfs in the *Snow White* movie, but he didn't do anything for "Alexander's Ragtime Band" that night. Lasky saw the splendid indifference with which it had been treated, and ordered it out of the show.

As consolation, he assured Berlin that he thought "Spanish Love" and "I Beg Your Pardon, Broadway" were great and would become all-time hits. But "Alexander's Ragtime Band"? In the words of his future brother-in-law, Sam Goldwyn, "Include me out."

Lasky later admitted that if he had had more sense, he'd have found a way to make a fortune out of that song. As it turned out, he lost a fortune on both the *International Revue* and on his Folies Bérgère.

Meanwhile, Snyder and Waterson were forming a new company and invited Berlin to join them as a partner. Since this meant that Berlin would now be a publisher in his own right, he was not going to let "Alexander" be consigned to oblivion.

To an entertainer, one of the most important factors of success is to be recognized as such by others in the business. In 1911, Berlin was invited to join the Friars Club. Still more of an honor, he was to be allowed to take part in one of their shows, a package always called the *Friars Frolic*.

All he had to do, he was told, was to produce a novelty. Instead of dreaming up a new number, he took "Alexander's Ragtime Band" out of the file and wrote a set of words to go with it. So it was at the *Frolic* that anyone first heard the words, "Come on and hear . . . come on and hear . . . Alexander's Ragtime Band." Berlin played his one-key piano in concert with a whole bunch of other songwriters all pounding the tune out on uprights. Among them was Harry Williams, who took part in the "Alexander" number after singing a hit of his own called "In the Shade of the Old Apple Tree."

The audience clapped earnestly but not enthusiastically.

Berlin was disappointed at the reception of his salvage operation but that night it did not matter too much. George M. Cohan was making a speech in his honor.

The great George M. allowed himself what some thought was a bad joke. "Irving Berlin," he said, "is a Jewboy who named himself after an English actor and a German city." There were those who thought he was betraying a touch of anti-Semitism, too—although Cohan's partner, Sam Harris, would never have agreed.

"Irvy writes a great song," Cohan proclaimed to the show biz successes around him. "A great song with a good lyric. It's music you don't have to dress up to listen to, but it is good music."

And then the master added, "He is a wonderful little fellow, wonderful in lots of ways. He has become famous and wealthy without wearing a lot of jewelry and falling for funny clothes. He is Uptown but he is there with the old Downtown hardshell. And with all his success, you will find his watch and his handkerchiefs in his pocket where they belong."

With that, "Irvy" played the piano again—"Alexander's Ragtime Band," of course.

He made sure that the artists who made the circuit of publishing houses were shown copies of "Alexander" as soon as they came into Waterson, Berlin and Snyder. One by one, under this persuasion, they considered what they could do with the tune.

Finally, a loud, deep-voiced, busty vaudeville entertainer named Emma Carus heard about the number, liked what she heard, and decided to sing it. From a stage in Chicago, she belted out the number. Anyone who heard it that night was sure never to forget the experience. The theater's chandeliers rocked with the ragtime beat. The walls reverberated with the sound of the audience's response.

A critic in the audience that night commented the next day in a Chicago newspaper, "If I were John D. Rockefeller or the Bank of England, I should engage the Coliseum and get a sextet including Caruso. After the sextet had sung it about ten times, we should have, as a finale, Sousa's Band march about the building, tearing the melody to pieces with variations."

At the same time, Al Jolson was singing "Alexander's Ragtime Band" from his end-man position in the lineup of Dockstader's Minstrels and was getting a similar response. Vaudevillians Eddie Miller and Helen Vincent performed it and were treated to hearing the audience react as though they had just been invited to a party with all the drinks on the house.

Berlin himself was invited to take a top-of-the-bill spot at Hammerstein's Victoria, playing all his own songs on the one-key piano. He wound up, of course, with "Alexander." Soon afterward, Carl Van Vechten wrote in the magazine *Vanity Fair,* "It's real American Music. Music of such vitality that it made the Grieg-Schumann-Wagner dilutions of Machovelli sound a little thin and the saccharine bars of Narcissus and Ophelia so much pseudo-Chaminade concocted in an American back parlor, while it completely routed the so-called art music of the professors."

Not long after the Emma Carus success, a youngster called George Gershwin was telling his teacher Charles Hambitzer, "This is American music. This is the way an American should write. This is the kind of music *I* want to write."

In the first three weeks after its Chicago debut, "Alexander's Ragtime Band" sold a million copies of sheet music. By the end of 1911, the figures had reached two million. *Variety* now referred to Irving Berlin as "Berlin the Hit-Maker."

Whether they were hits or not, though, Irving Berlin's output of songs in 1911 was prodigious. Besides "Alexander," he churned out songs with titles ranging from "Yiddisha Nightingale" and "Yiddle on Your Fiddle" (copyrighted the year before) to "Goodbye Becky Cohen" and "That Kazzatsky Dance." He also wrote "When You Kiss an Italian Girl," "Antonia, You'd Better Come Home," "My Sweet Italian Man," and "Dat's-a My Gal," the last a dialect song *par excellence.*

But ragtime was the order of the day. Society hostesses were jettisoning the waltz and allowing the orchestras they imported into their salons to play ragtime. Yale University banned the music, which only served to make it the more attractive to students. Football cheerleaders whipped up encouragement in ragtime. Dance studios began specializing in ragtime lessons.

And Irving Berlin went on supplying the music. He produced "Everybody's Doin' It" that same year, and it became almost as classic as "Alexander." A year or so before, Eddie Cantor had first been noticed on Broadway, singing "My Wife's Gone to the Country." He hadn't yet been called "Banjo Eyes" but he was on his way to success. Now Berlin had a new song for him, "Ragtime Violin."

Everyone was talking about "Irving Berlin, the Ragtime King." Not all the talk was kind, however. It was about this time that the rumor started making the rounds of Tin Pan Alley: Berlin was paying a young Negro—"his little black boy," the story went—to turn out tunes on his behalf, and always under the Berlin name. How else, the gossips buzzed, could he be so successful at creating music that was straight from Dixie?

Every time Berlin had a new hit, the story surfaced again. At first Berlin ignored it, but he became less and less indulgent the more often he heard it. Fortunately for both him and the music business, none of the people who mattered took it seriously.

There were also stories of entertainers actually fighting to get to his material first. According to an anecdote he told years later to Eric Bennett in the *London Sunday Chronicle,* two girls came to blows in his own office. The newspaper article quoted Berlin, "She leaned across the desk to plead for it. But she had hardly begun to speak when another Broadway adorable swept into the room. As soon as she heard what the first girl was asking, she rushed across to the desk, pulling her away, shouting, 'No! *I* want it.' "

According to the article, the first girl was Dorothy Goetz, a sister of E. Ray Goetz, one of Berlin's closest friends. Together they had written a Mexican number called "Sombrero Land," with Berlin supplying the tune and his friend the lyrics. Two of their others were "Yankee Love" and "Don't Take Your Beau to the Seashore."

Because of his association with Ray, Berlin had come to know his beautiful young sister.

In the *Sunday Chronicle* story, Bennett said Berlin told him, "Dorothy was a woman of spirit. She swung around a haymaking left and slapped the newcomer across the face. The two closed, swapping punches like a couple of prize-ring veterans, and I was powerless to separate them. They were scratching, tearing hair and shouting in lovely voices that they wanted to sing my song. Well, I had dreamed of people fighting for the right to sing my stuff, but this was the first time I saw that dream come true."

Dorothy did not get the song. But she did get a date with Irving Berlin.

By 1912, less than four years after "Marie from Sunny Italy," Berlin had made $100,000 in royalties. He enjoyed his newly successful position but he did not forget his past. He drew up in a taxi one day outside the East Side apartment where his mother now lived. Berlin got out and raced up the stairs. Leah was busy in the kitchen but stopped to give her Izzy a loving hug.

"I want you to come for a ride," he told his mother in Yiddish.

"I can't," she protested, "I have to get supper."

"Forget supper," he said. "There's something I want to show you." So Leah took her hat and coat and walked down the stairs with her son to sit in the back of the gleaming cab. They drove through the streets of the East Side. And then out of the tenement area to the sight of trees and green fields. They drew up in front of a large house with its own steps leading up to its own front door.

"Where's this, Izzy?" she asked.

"The Bronx," he told her. Mrs. Baline knew that the Bronx was where the fancy Jews lived, not at all the sort of people she had ever mixed with.

Berlin beckoned his mother to get out of the car and follow

him up the steps to the door. A servant answered their knock.

Through the hall they walked, past one room and then another. In the living room, Leah sat down only when Berlin insisted.

"But what is this?" she protested. "I've got to get back home to make supper."

"You don't have to get supper tonight, Ma," he said, and gave her a big kiss.

Only then did the truth dawn on Leah Baline. Minutes later, the maid who had greeted them at the front door came into the room and announced that dinner was served.

"It's all yours, Ma," Berlin told her. "This is home now."

Supper had been cooked in advance. There was not only a maid in the smart new house in the Bronx but a kosher cook, too.

Mrs. Baline was as proud as she was pleased. But like all other mothers of the time, she wanted just one more thing from her son: that he settle down and marry a nice Jewish girl and produce children. She knew he had a girlfriend. Her name was Dorothy, but Leah had not been told any more and did not ask.

In 1910, Berlin reflected on the hit he had made with "My Wife's Gone to the Country."

"The public wants to have some fun with marriage," he said. "Get up a song panning the husband or the wife. Show up some of the little funny streaks in domestic life and your fortune is made, at least for the moment. What the public likes one minute, it tires of the next."

Berlin himself was in love. It might lead to a chance to see what the "funny streaks in domestic life" really were.

5

When I Lost You

IRVING AND DOROTHY GOETZ fell in love soon after their first meeting. When they announced their engagement, the showmen of Broadway and the music makers of Tin Pan Alley showered them with congratulations.

Leah Baline's congratulations were more muted. She was sorry that her Izzy, son of a cantor, had chosen to marry outside his faith. But she understood and forgave.

They married in 1912, with all the world agog over the lovers. Their seemingly idyllic honeymoon in Cuba would one day be the inspiration of a song called "I'll See You in C-U-B-A."

But the reality in Cuba belied their impression. The young newlyweds—he was only twenty-four, she was just twenty—had arrived on the island just before typhoid broke out. They returned to a new apartment in the smartest part of the city to plan and to decorate. After all, Riverside Drive, overlooking the Hudson River, was going to be where their children would be born. All was bustle. Irving had installed his one-key piano and was busy trying to work on tunes, but decorators ran about with wallpaper rolls, pots of paint, stepladders, and planks.

But soon, in the midst of it, there was also a team of doctors and nurses. Dorothy was seriously ill, a victim of typhoid. Specialists were called in. They tried and fought. But one day the look on Irving's face told callers from Tin Pan Alley what they had

41

most feared: five months after her honeymoon, Dorothy, the beautiful girl Irving had courted and won, was dead.

Berlin's grief was deep and black. He tried to write, but sounds made no sense, words conveyed no feeling.

Dorothy's brother Ray tried to take his brother-in-law out of a misery into which he also had plunged. One day he came to Berlin with a couple of steamship tickets. "We're going to Europe," he announced.

It was Berlin's first trip to the Continent since his father and mother had brought him from there. If he had felt frightened in 1892, he felt just as lonely, worried, and miserable in 1912. The bottom had fallen out of his world; without Dorothy to inspire him, the career that had promised so much was at an end.

When the two men returned from Europe, Berlin tried again to write. But still there was no fire in the music, no love or soul in the words. It was then that Ray told him not to try to forget his troubles, but to exploit them. "You're a man who writes from your emotions," he told him. "Let your emotions work for you."

What on the surface seemed a callous suggestion turned out to be the best therapy Irving Berlin could have had. He sat at the piano and let his heart pour out into a song called "When I Lost You." Within a week or so after Waterson, Berlin and Snyder had printed it, the song had sold a million copies. All over the country, young men warbled the song to weeping wives. George M. Cohan called it "the prettiest song I've ever heard in my life."

"When I Lost You" was the first real ballad by a man who was soon to be accepted as America's Number One Balladeer. But he was not confining himself to the romantic song. A big 1913 hit was "When the Midnight Choo-Choo Leaves for Alabam." Not such a big hit was a song which Fay Templeton introduced in the Weber and Fields show *Hokey Pokey*—a parody Berlin himself wrote called "Alexander's Bagpipe Band."

Berlin's work was the subject now of frequent analysis in newspapers and magazines. *Greenbook Magazine* was fascinated to discover, "As with George M. Cohan, the second verse of a song is Berlin's bugbear. With the melody and the first verse and refrain written, Berlin's interest cools and he is eager to get to work on a new idea."

The idea that interested him most at this time was an offer from Albert de Courville in England to star at his London Hippodrome, then one of the biggest variety houses in the capital. He would play and sing his own songs.

On this Atlantic crossing, Berlin did something he repeated on every subsequent trip abroad: he used the journey to write a song, dictating it to the musical secretary he took with him on all his voyages. He called the new song "The International Rag." When he introduced it from the stage of the Hippodrome, the audience reaction made him feel he had earned his billing as "The King of Ragtime." His "subjects" begged for more, shouting out requests one after another. Berlin played whatever they wanted.

That night in London did more for Irving Berlin than anything he had ever before experienced as a songwriter. The triumph of "Alexander's Ragtime Band" had come to him second-hand because the first person to really hear applause for the number was Emma Carus. "When I Lost You" had sold a million copies. Yet none of the money that came flooding in from that tune was compensation for what he had really lost. But in the Hippodrome Theatre they were shouting for Irving Berlin himself. In those cheers he was, for the first time, able to bury some of his grief.

The realization of the impact he'd had on England came to him one afternoon as he was helped out of a cab. The doorman, the moment he opened the car door, began whistling "Alexander's Ragtime Band." The young passenger was so moved by this sign of instant recognition that he gave the porter a gold sovereign.

On June 19, 1913, the *London Daily Express* was enthused about the "genius who dictates his syncopated melodies." They revealed his earnings of twenty thousand pounds a year. The *Express* rhapsodized: "Go where you will, you cannot escape from the mazes of music he has spun. In every London restaurant, park and theatre you hear his strains. Paris dances to them. Berlin sips golden beer to his melodies. Vienna has forsaken the waltz, Madrid flung away her castanets and Venice forgotten her barcarolles. Ragtime," the piece went on, recording history as it happened, "has swept like a whirlwind over the earth and set civilization humming."

The final reason for the paper's amazement was that Berlin had done so much so soon. He was just twenty-five.

When Berlin returned to the United States, he was grateful to see that he had not been forgotten by his fellow countrymen. People were actually taking excursion trips down to Tin Pan Alley in the hope that they might spot Berlin walking on the street with a colleague. Not that he was all that happy about being recognized by strangers. If someone from the Bowery called out "Izzy," he'd turn around and greet an old friend warmly. But being accosted by someone he didn't know would only drive him into a shell of shyness.

He was nervous, intense, prolific. His arranger was kept busy with "In My Harem" to which World War I soldiers later sang unprintable lyrics of their own; "Rum Tum Tiddle," which marked Al Jolson's recording debut; and a piece of nonsense called "If You Don't Want My Peaches You Better Stop Shaking My Tree."

The great Florenz Ziegfeld featured Berlin songs in his Ziegfeld Follies. Other producers ordered new Berlin songs as though they were telephoning for groceries. On one occasion an urgent message came to him in Chicago that Waterson and Snyder wanted him to call New York.

"We've got to have a song fast," said Harry Waterson.

"Right," said Berlin. "Let me think . . ." And then and there on the telephone he sang them the new ragtime ditty they needed for someone's musical.

He told friends that inspiration came at any time, in any place. Some of his best ideas—"Alexander's Ragtime Band" was one—he got while shaving. Others came in the bath or while he was out walking. Rarely were they the result of just sitting poised over his one-key piano, staring at F sharp or the lever beneath the keyboard.

Sitting down to work, he looked like any other boss dictating to a secretary, except that Berlin dictated in a series of hums and plonks and his secretary jotted on music paper instead of a steno pad. Of course he was sometimes inspired in the middle of the night, when there was no music secretary to be called. Then he used a Dictaphone. He would take out the machine and sing "until the cylinder choked with syncopation." If driven to it, he could produce a new song every day of the week, but his average was one finished piece a week.

Charles B. Dillingham approached him with an idea for writing a full-scale musical and the idea excited him. Before this, he had had thoughts of writing his own opera. "It will be a grand opera in ragtime," he had told reporters. "Not a musical comedy but a real opera on a tragic theme." Although these thoughts would recur from time to time, just as a clown might dream of playing Hamlet, he directed his attention to Charles Dillingham.

Dillingham was one of Broadway's great impresarios. He put himself in the same league as the Shubert brothers and Ziegfeld, and his ambitions were no less grand. He wanted to produce the first big ragtime musical, so of course he wanted the first big ragtime composer.

Besides the musical numbers, *Watch Your Step* was going to have lavish sets, and the dance team of Vernon and Irene Castle would be making their Broadway debut.

Berlin came up with twenty new songs. Some were instantly forgotten. But many others were remembered, not just long enough for the carriage ride home, but for generations after. The show kept people coming to the New Amsterdam Theater for months. One of its hits was the lilting "Syncopated Walk," which the Castles made famous. Another far more enduring success was "Play a Simple Melody," Berlin's first duet. The melody was far

from simple, but it remains one of his best songs. People like Bing
Crosby, Ethel Merman, and Jean Sablon scored hits with it right
up to the 1960s.

One of the show's numbers seemed to be the result of a Berlin
twinge of conscience. Called "Opera Burlesque," it turned out to
be the nearest he ever got to writing that dream opera. It ran to
seventeen pages of sheet music and featured a tortured figure of
Verdi appealing angrily to tunesmiths like Berlin not to write
parodies of his great arias.

Watch Your Step heralded the era when an Irving Berlin
score for a production transformed it instantly into an Irving
Berlin show. His name was more important now than any star's.
Wrote one critic when the show opened, "More than to anyone
else, 'Watch Your Step' belongs to Irving Berlin."

The Friars Club gave another dinner in his honor, and once
more George M. Cohan was there to make a speech.

Meanwhile, Berlin's rivals changed the story of the little black
boy to "a slave kept locked up in a back room." When the one
slave became three slaves locked up in the back room, Berlin
joined in the laughter.

In 1914, thirty-five places were laid for New York's top
songwriters at Lüchow's Restaurant. Only nine of the invited
turned up, Victor Herbert among them. The rest, including
Jerome Kern, Max Dreyfus, and Berlin, refused to accept. They
did not like the idea of the nine to form a "trade union" of songwriters. But the organization was set up despite them: the American Society of Composers, Authors, and Publishers, or, as everyone in the business now knows it, ASCAP. Before long, many of
the absentees joined up. But at the time, most everybody
seemed happy with making progress on his own.

When Berlin knew he had a good tune, he would get on the
telephone as soon as he got off the piano stool. Generally, he
would try to call Al Jolson first, particularly if it were a popular
song that needed a bit of emotion to put it over.

"Al, I've got a tune just made for you," he'd say, and Jolson would send for the piece as soon as it had been polished. Berlin always had a soft spot for, but a clear head about, Jolson. "I got to know him very well," he told me. "He was a man who was always very generous. With his talent."

Berlin's piano was like a slot machine: as soon as he pulled the lever, he would as often as not hit the jackpot. There were, it is true, some exceptions. In 1914, he wrote a tune called "Stay Down Here Where You Belong." Today, he says, "You can blackmail me with that one." And Groucho Marx does it regularly. "Every time I see him," Berlin says, "I stick my hand in my pocket and ask him, 'How much if you don't sing that . . . ?' "

If it were a comic song, Berlin would direct it to Belle Baker, who had sung Berlin's "Cohen Owes Me Ninety-seven Dollars," and as a result was more than comfortably well-off. Really big entertainers would get Mr. Berlin's personal attention when they wanted something tailor-made to their own talents. Others would simply try to get what they could from "stock."

Among the unknowns was a young dance team who called at the Waterson, Berlin and Snyder offices wanting a new number. They did not get to see Berlin himself. "After all, we were just a couple of kids," Fred Astaire recalls now. But he and his sister Adele did manage to buy a tune called "I Love to Quarrel with You" which they featured in their vaudeville "child" act.

By the end of 1915, Broadway was crowded with war plays. There was even one at that temple of vaudeville, the Palace, taking up part of what was normally a solid variety bill. It was called *The Spoils of War*. In it a lady called Helen Rook sang a Berlin song that Al Jolson soon adopted as his own, "When I Leave the World Behind."

Jolson was devoted to it, but the song had actually been dedicated by Berlin to someone he'd never known. Berlin had read in a magazine about a Chicago lawyer named Charles Lounsbery, whose strange will had included the clause, "I leave to children exclusively, but only for the lifetime of their childhood, all and every, the dandelions of the field and the daisies thereof."

The story was that Lounsbery was a poor man for whom the best things in life were free (to borrow a phrase from a set of songwriters called De Sylva, Brown, and Henderson). Berlin pondered the story and then wrote a song about the moonlight being left to lovers and birds being bequeathed to sing to the blind. He inscribed the early copies of "When I Leave the World Behind" to "the memory of Charles Lounsbery, whose will suggested the theme for this song."

Years later, the will was discovered to have been a work of fiction. It had been contributed to a banker's magazine by a man named Willston Fish. But the "will"—like the song Berlin had written—had impressed a lot of people.

Although Berlin sought to keep his private life to himself, his fame as a public figure spread far beyond Tin Pan Alley and Broadway, his usual haunts.

An Italian newspaper reported that Giacomo Puccini wanted to collaborate with him if he ever decided to write his ragtime opera. The two never made any direct arrangements, but Ray Goetz did meet with Puccini, and they discussed the idea.

Writing such an opera was for Berlin an intriguing possibility. In 1916 he told the *New York Times,* "You can repeat 'I love you' a number of times in syncopated measure very effectively, whereas if you used the ordinary forms it would sound simple.

"If I were assigned the task of writing an American opera, I should not follow the style of the masters, whose melodies can never be surpassed. Instead, I would write a syncopated opera which, if it failed, would at least possess the merit of novelty. That is what I really want to do eventually." But he never did. He was most content to write popular songs which, he told the *Times,* he enjoyed even more than the scores of shows.

In 1915, at New York's Globe Theatre, there was a new Berlin score for a new Dillingham show, *Stop! Look! Listen!* It starred

Gaby Deslys, the French beauty who had been introduced to Broadway audiences in the first Al Jolson shows at the Winter Garden, along with Harry Pilcer, Blossom Seeley, Marion Harris, and a host of others. But above all, once more, there was the memorable Berlin score, including "The Girl on the Magazine Cover" and "I Love a Piano."

A life-size portrait of Berlin had been hung in the Globe Theatre lobby. But it didn't stay there long: some of his old singing-waiter colleagues stole it to take back to the Bowery with them. He considered it a nice tribute indeed.

In 1916, Berlin went back to London. He stayed at the Savoy Hotel and bought a forty-volume Shakespeare collection at an auction there. "It sounds as if a selection from *The Taming of the Shrew* is going to be done in jig time," quipped the *New York World,* without knowing it was beating Cole Porter to an idea by more than forty years. That particular idea didn't strike Berlin.

But it had occurred to Waterson, Berlin and Snyder that since not everyone could go to theaters or vaudeville houses, the music publishers somehow had to go to the people. So they thought about using advertising techniques. They picked a new Berlin tune called "Smile and Show Your Dimple" as a test case. Philadelphia was chosen for this marketing operation and the city was flooded with newspaper advertisements. Every big store window in the city was covered with posters. Newsboys were hired to deliver circulars, and sandwich-boardmen walked through the streets with declarations that the wonderful Irving Berlin had written a wonderful new tune and sheet music was now available for purchase.

Tin Pan Alley executives predicted that "Smile and Show Your Dimple" would sell overnight by the hundred thousands. But almost no one smiled and not a dimple was creased. Only 2,500 copies of the song actually sold.

It was a salutory lesson which proved one thing beyond doubt: even the name Irving Berlin was not good enough to sell a song unheard. It also proved how good his other tunes must have been to sell entirely on their own merits. As for "Smile and Show Your Dimple," it was put away in the files, ready to be dusted off seventeen years later with a new name, "Easter Parade."

Meanwhile, dozens of young men knocked at the door of Waterson, Berlin and Snyder, asking not merely for advice on how to write songs, but for jobs as apprentices to the master. One of them was a youngster whose background was not very different from Berlin's own. He was dark, Jewish, born on New York's lower East Side of immigrant parents, and he desperately wanted to write music.

Somehow or other—and such things were not easy—he managed to get to a piano in the publishers' office just as Berlin came in the door and could hear him play. He played a couple of tunes he had written himself.

"Not bad," said Berlin. "I'd say you had some talent." The boy was there long enough to hear Berlin hum a tune. Having listened, the youngster was able to play it straight back to him.

Berlin was impressed. "You can have a job as an arranger and musical secretary," he told the boy. "What's your name?"

"George Gershvine," the youngster replied, and gladly accepted the job.

"Don't take my job offer," Berlin advised Gershvine. "You've got more talent than an arranger needs."

"Yes," the youngster agreed, "perhaps I have." And he went to work as a rehearsal pianist. He made his own way to the top, of course. But for George Gershwin, Irving Berlin always remained America's Franz Schubert.

The year of young Gershwin's visit, Berlin was asked by Florenz Ziegfeld to help him out of a jam. Ziegfeld had just taken over the Century Theatre, a showplace with a name for itself that was not altogether nice. To give a different dazzle to its reputation, Ziegfeld brought in Irving Berlin and Victor Herbert to write the music for his new extravaganza, *The Century Girl*. Each man wrote about half the songs for the show, one often consulting the other for ideas.

When the job was finally done the two songwriters went off to the Lambs Club to celebrate. Berlin was proud to have worked with a man like Herbert and a little in awe of him too, as he always was in the presence of composers who had had professional training for their careers.

"Victor," Berlin asked, "people say that if I studied music, it would overwhelm me. Do you agree with them?"

To which Herbert replied, "Irving, you have a natural talent for putting music and words together. Mind you, a little science wouldn't hurt."

Berlin decided the time had come to take music lessons. He would then no longer need to dictate his tunes. He might even be able to play one of the grand pianos he had bought but which were no more than ornamental furniture.

It didn't work out that way. As he told me, "I was never a good student. I was much too impatient. I studied and practiced for two days and then gave it up. I realized I could have written two songs and made myself some money in that time."

He was once asked what effect education might have had on his music. His answer was instant. "Ruin it," he said.

If anyone looked set to ruin his career in 1917 it was probably the Kaiser. America had entered the war and the country was steeped in patriotic fervor. Irving Berlin volunteered to entertain the troops. But the matter was taken out of his hands without the chance of singing to a single serviceman.

The *Toledo Blade* put it in one simple headline: "United States Takes Berlin."

6

Oh, How I Hate to Get Up in the Morning

ONCE THE U.S. ENTERED the war, of course, Berlin reflected on the demands it made of a songwriter.

"I don't believe the boys in France want sad, tearful songs about dying in the battlefield or patriotic discourses about being on duty and going to lick the Kaiser," he wrote, "because they do these things as part of the day's work. The trouble with most of our sentimental ballads is that they haven't any real connection with the war. They are tearful songs about absent loved ones who might just as well be in Milwaukee or Hong Kong as far as any real connection with war is concerned. I hope we shall have something better."

Pondering the production of that "something better," he received the draft notice. Mr. Berlin was invited to report to Camp Upton at Fort Yaphank on Long Island.

At Upton he found that he was expected to listen to music (the bugler's) rather than play it. He listened and made his bunk and swept floors, discovering what the world looked like at five o'clock in the morning. What it looked like to him was upside down.

A man who often wrote his best songs at night or went to Manhattan's socialite parties frequently saw five o'clock in the morning, but only as a time to think about going to bed. Now he saw what it was like to get up at five o'clock, and what he saw he didn't like.

From the moment the headline appeared in the *Toledo Blade*, it was obvious that Berlin was going to be something of a celebrity at Fort Yaphank, if the non-commissioned officers gave him a chance. Certainly his bunkmates were impressed to have him among them. Hardly a draftee's first letter home could have gone without mention of his presence.

Berlin never consciously walked around as a celebrity, but there were sergeants and perhaps even captains who relished the idea of taking him down a peg or two with reminders of who was now boss. So Private Berlin did K.P. duty, swept more floors, and tried to learn which end of the gun was which.

Back on Broadway, George M. Cohan was paying tribute to him in his *Cohan Revue of 1918* by featuring a bundle of Berlin songs. They included the "Wedding of Words and Music" and another in which Cohan's music married Berlin's words, "Polly, Pretty Polly." Nora Bayes was the star of the show. Berlin had rewritten much of the material that had been penned for her by other writers. He had also contributed half the songs in another revue called *Dance and Grow Thin*. Al Jolson was singing his "From Here to Shanghai," and John McCormack recorded "Dream On, Little Soldier Boy."

Despite bugle calls and K.P., Irving had been quietly nourishing the idea of writing a show for the men with whom he now shared life. Curiously enough, most of his buddies were being posted to France, while Private Berlin went on sweeping floors. Then suddenly he found himself promoted to sergeant, and at the same time summoned to the quarters of the Commanding Officer, Major General J. Franklin Bell.

"I think we have a job for you," said the General. The new sergeant stood expectantly. "We want a community house, a place where friends and relatives of the men can be made more comfortable when they come to visit. It will cost money, of course, perhaps $35,000. We thought perhaps you could put on a little show to make that money."

Could he ever!

General Bell asked what Berlin wanted. Within a few days a committee of three officers was set up to see that whatever Berlin demanded, he got. He would need no fewer than three hundred men, half of them to appear in the show, the rest to play in the orchestra, and act as stage managers, property men, scenery designers and painters. If they weren't professionally trained, they must be extremely talented. No halfway measures, please.

One stipulation made by General Bell and his committee was that since this was to be an Army show about Army people, there could be no women allowed. But because servicemen thought about women more than they thought about practically anything else, there would have to be references to women at least; women in comedy routines, maybe, and—well, why not?—women singing and dancing. The women, of course, would have to be played by men.

Men came to auditions and went, heard and unwanted. The talent Irving intended to assemble was going to be not just good, but superb. There had been Army shows before, but they'd generally been no more than a step up, sometimes even a step down, from the entertainment of a church social. This was to be the greatest Army show of all time.

In June 1918, Berlin announced that he was ready. He had booked the show into Broadway's Century Theatre, where two years before he and Victor Herbert had cooperated on Ziegfeld's *Century Girl.* The new show, called *Yip Yip Yaphank*, was scheduled to run for eight performances.

A massive publicity campaign was mounted; posters were widely distributed; New York newspapers ran advertisements; and seats went on sale at fifty cents to two dollars.

The entertainment world of Broadway was quick to catch on to the idea of the show. A month before the Century Theatre opening, Sergeant Berlin organized a preview of selections at the camp's own little theatrical hall. A special train brought more than seventy actors and Broadway performers over for the show. Among them were Al Jolson, Fanny Brice, Will Rogers, Eddie

Cantor, and Harry Fox (the man who introduced "I'm Always Chasing Rainbows"). There was also a chorus of girls from Broadway's *Midnight Frolics*. They went over particularly well with the Yaphankers, who realized that they wouldn't see anything quite like them at the Century.

For this preview, Sergeant Berlin had an orchestra, six pianos, and a double quartet of soldiers singing. To win Authority's everlasting support, they sang two numbers specially written about General Bell. At the end of the concert, just before Al Jolson led the artists to a reception in the officers' club, General Bell made a speech of genuine gratitude to all the stage folk.

At the Century Theatre, the curtain went up on *Yip Yip Yaphank* in August, and the *New York Times* pronounced it "A Rousing Hit."

A rousing hit indeed it was. There had never been a Service show like it. The comedians were top comics, the dancers stepped out on stage as though they had been born to it, and the singers hit not a sour note.

Audiences at soldier shows expected to make allowances and to clap out of kindness. The shouts of approval after each act came because the people out front—those in officers' uniforms as well as tuxedos, those who came as enlisted men with their wives and girlfriends, those who were clerks and arms factory workers having an evening out—were enjoying themselves as never before.

They loved the Berlin tunes and particularly cheered the debut of "Mandy," performed as a minstrel number. It was sung by a chorus of servicemen in blackface, dressed as little girls with white ribbons in their hair. "Mandy" herself was Private Dan Healy. There were friendly but intentionally derisory shouts from the audience when a chorus began to sing "I Can Always Find a Little Sunshine in the YMCA," but the derision turned to warmth as soon as they realized what a beautiful piece of barbershop music it was.

Nothing, though, drew wilder applause than the lone figure of a soldier, standing in an ill-fitting Army tunic, Boy Scout type of hat firmly in place. It was Sergeant Berlin himself. He sang two numbers that had the heart of every serviceman present that night: "Poor Little Me—I'm on K.P." was one. "I scrub the dishes against my wishes," he wailed. The other song was probably the most heartfelt thing he had written since "When I Lost You." It was called "Oh, How I Hate to Get Up in the Morning." The audience stood and cheered for minutes. With almost every number, members of the audience laughed as they never had before.

Commented the *New York Times,* "The chorus of *Yip Yip Yaphank* is guaranteed to be one long laugh whether one regards the third from the left, the fourth from the right, or the ensemble in general. Whoever picked its members was nothing less than inspired. And that, of course, was Berlin, who even found Benny Leonard, World Lightweight Champion, in uniform somewhere and brought him into the show to give a boxing demonstration."

Even with all this talent, however, the *Times* admitted, "The show does not depend on such obvious merit. It is at its best when the music is playing, for Berlin is first and foremost a songwriter." Of the songs, the *Times* writer prophesied: "Most of them will soon probably be more than familiar, for they are certain to find their way into vaudeville and musical comedy."

The show's finale was "We're on Our Way to France," which brought more than a few tears out front. The *Times* called it "a patriotic number." There would have been another patriotic number called "God Bless America," but Berlin thought about it and ordered it out. "It seemed a little like gilding the lily to have soldiers sing it," said Berlin, and buried it in his files.

At the end of the first night, General Bell made another speech of appreciation, standing in the box from which he had watched the show. He called on Sergeant Berlin to speak, but Berlin was too shy to come out and talk. His "speeches" had been made all evening and were a lot more effective than the General's had been.

Berlin did, however, allow himself to be hoisted shoulder-high by the rest of the cast while the entire audience thundered applause. Every member of the audience, that is, except one. In another box was Berlin's mother. Since Leah could understand so little of anything but Yiddish, she had missed most of the show's meaning. But she kept her feelings to herself until she got home to the Bronx. It was then that she confessed to her son that she had never been so upset, so frightened. She was amazed he had been let off.

"Let off, Mama?" he asked her incredulously.

"Yes, by all the gangsters who got hold of you and carried you on their shoulders. However did you escape?"

The show was supposed to have lasted for eight performances. At the end of six weeks, the press was still running advertisements for "*Yip Yip Yaphank*—Sergeant Irving Berlin and his Boys." (The Army had wanted $35,000. Sergeant Berlin presented them with a check for $83,000.)

The thirty-second performance, the final night, was a truly emotional one. The show came to an end, not because audiences were no longer jamming into every seat that could be found at the Century Theatre, but because the War Department had decided that the men could do more good behind battlelines. That night, as the full company sang, "We're on Our Way to France," they really were. The entire cast, all the actors, dancers, singers, directors, and carpenters split into two lines with Irving Berlin himself at the head of one, and walked off the stage—half of them going down steps to the right, the other half to the left. Then, coming together at the center aisle, they marched out of the theatre, into the street, and to a waiting troop transport.

At first the audience thought it was part of the show. When they began to suspect that this was something real, they stood up dumbfounded . . . and with dawning realization let the tears flow.

None of the men in the *Yip Yip Yaphank* company, even Sergeant Berlin, knew whether they would ever play before an audience again. But two months later, the war that had been going so badly was over and won.

7

Shaking the Blues Away

W HEN B ERLIN HUNG UP his khaki uniform for the last time in 1919, he had a sly dig ready for the people who had first greeted him at Camp Upton. "I've Got My Captain Working for Me Now," sang Al Jolson, and thousands of young veterans, returning to the job market, relished the sentiment enough to turn the song into a hit.

For other servicemen, of course, the wounded and the maimed, the end of the war signalled no more than the beginnings of helplessness. All over the country money was being raised for veterans' aid. Broadway did its part with benefit performances, the casts often appealing directly from the stage to their audiences.

Irving Berlin was sitting out front watching a performance of *39 East* at the Broadhurst Theatre one night when he was recognized by someone sitting nearby. The man stood up and announced his "find" to the rest of the audience. There were cheers throughout the house, and Berlin sank further into his seat, thoroughly embarrassed. But the man went on: "I'll give five hundred dollars to the Salvation Army if Mr. Berlin will sing to us. . . ."

Mr. Berlin was even more uncomfortable. Essentially a salesman, he was paradoxically shy. He sang his own songs because he liked to, but he always had to prepare himself for the prospect. Yet this was a challenge he could hardly escape. How could he deprive the Salvation Army of five hundred dollars?

So he mounted the stage and sang "Oh, How I Hate to Get Up in the Morning."

The fan didn't rest. "I'll give another five hundred dollars for one more chorus." The audience roared its approbation of the idea, so Berlin, croaking a bit, went on singing for the Salvation Army's gain.

There were others who gained from his music. During the war, Captain Eddie Rickenbacker's squadron had used a Berlin tune as its own anthem. "If I Had My Way I'd Live Among the Gypsies," written originally as a background piece for a Douglas Fairbanks movie, it was taken up by the "Hat-in-the-Ring" squadron boys and Berlin quite forgot about it. But a youngster named Cole Porter heard it in France, sang it while driving ambulances and giving camp shows along the length of the Western Front, and then played it to his society friends back home once he was out of uniform. Not until Berlin was asked for permission to use the number in a movie being made about Rickenbacker did he remember he had written it.

His output was phenomenal: songs that simply came to him as well as those made to order for Broadway shows—Cohan's *Royal Vagabond*, Julia Sanderson's *The Canary*. As often as not, he sat up all night working on something during a fit of insomnia.

His best writing actually came when there was a deadline to meet, when either Waterson or Snyder pointed out that the firm needed one or another kind of tune to fill an order. He would sit at his piano, obstinately hitting those black keys until thought—he never liked the word inspiration—produced the required love ballad or comedy song or incidental ditty or specialty number.

It was a time when people sang about their mothers, so Berlin came up with "The Hand That Rocked My Cradle Rules My Heart" and followed it with "Was There Ever a Pal Like You?" If there were fathers who felt jealous, Berlin had solace for them—"I Left My Door Open and My Daddy Walked Out." It was a time when women were shocking male society with their campaign for equality, so Berlin gave his public "Everything Is Rosy Now for Rosie" and "Since Katy the Waitress Became an Aviatress."

Berlin the businessman was every bit as competent as Berlin the composer. And it was the businessman in him that decided to part company with the two men who had helped launch his already fantastic career. He withdrew from the Waterson, Berlin and Snyder enterprise to form Irving Berlin Inc., his own publishing company. Now he would have to nag himself to meet deadlines.

It could have been a risky business—throwing away guaranteed profits of an established concern. It could have been, but it wasn't. Still creating new songs, he began buying back as many of his old ones as he could. Amassing copyrights, he eventually amassed additional fortunes.

Florenz Ziegfeld, considering the 1919 edition of his Follies, decided on all-out expense. He would spare nothing to get the biggest and best and brightest of stars. There would be opulence to every set, every costume. The Ziegfeld Girls would be magnificent—taller, curvier, more beautiful than ever. And Irving Berlin would do the score.

It was the very splendor of the girls that presented Berlin with a deadline problem. Four days before the show's opening, Ziegfeld asked for a special song, one that need do no more than help put across the beauty of the girls. Berlin was puzzled. Why on earth did that take help? The truth was that Ziegfeld, in a fit of more extravagance than usual, had bought dozens of costumes with no place in his show to use them. "My bookkeeper will kill me," he told Berlin. "Please help." It was an order from a client.

Berlin stayed up that night to think and the next day was back with a tune that has since become the stereotyped accompaniment to a beauty's suddenly stepping out of a picture frame: "A Pretty Girl Is Like a Melody." John Steel sang the number behind footlights while the Ziegfeld Girls came on stage, each representing a different melody by other composers. Hazel Washburn was "Spring Song," Martha Pierre was "Elegy," Jessie Reed was "Barcarolle," Alta King, "Serenade," and Margaret Irving, "Träumerei."

For this Follies, Berlin revived "Mandy," the minstrel number that had been so popular in *Yip Yip Yaphank*. Gus Van and Joe Schenck sang it with Marilyn Miller, who later achieved further fame when she sang Jerome Kern's "Silver Lining." "End men" artists in the minstrel show were Eddie Cantor and Bert Williams (a fair-skinned Negro who blacked his face to make himself look more like the unreal, innocent caricature that the minstrel represented). Cantor had a new number which he later took as his own: "You'd Be Surprised." Perhaps even Berlin was surprised at just how successful that turned out to be.

During the Follies year, Berlin was invited, together with John McCormack and John Philip Sousa, to judge entries in a song contest sponsored by the *New York American*. First prize in the competition was $50,000. Once the professionals had picked that winner and other lesser ones, they decided that a tune called "Oh Land of Mine" had a certain merit, not great, but it seemed to justify the lowest prize, fifty dollars, they had to offer its anonymous writer. Only afterward did they discover that the composer had a name already well known in the song business. It was George Gershwin, the man who had just written "Swanee," the man who might once have been apprenticed to the writer of "Mandy."

Berlin the businessman was quite shrewd enough to recognize that other people's talents could help him make money. Soon after Irving Berlin Inc. opened, the principal of the firm was joined by a new partner, Walter Donaldson. Donaldson was the composer of Al Jolson's "My Mammy" and "Carolina in the Morning," and of Eddie Cantor's post-World War I hit, "How're Ya Gonna Keep 'Em Down on the Farm?"

Uppermost on America's mind in 1920 was the Volstead Act, known to some as the noble experiment, to everyone else as Prohibition. There was bathtub gin and there were speakeasies, but there were also places outside the dry United States where the rich could drink plentifully and legally. One of these havens was just ninety miles or so off the coast of Florida. And Irving Berlin had it in mind when he produced one of the really big hits of 1920, "I'll See You in C-U-B-A." It was only twelve years after the honeymoon that had ended in tragedy.

Once more, for Ziegfeld, Berlin tried to repeat the success of "A Pretty Girl Is Like a Melody" to be sung by John Steel, but "The Girls of My Dreams" was not so memorable. A non-show item of the same period, "After You Get What You Want, You Don't Want It," wasn't much of anything until the 1950s, when a young sensation named Marilyn Monroe sang it. At the time the song was written, Berlin confessed to the *Christian Science Monitor,* "It is much more difficult for me to write successes now because people expect so much from me on account of my previous hits."

Success bred other problems for him. He and eight other music publishers had got together to settle the prices at which they would sell piano rolls. The importance of that side of the business was not inconsiderable. A Berlin song of the twenties selling over a million phonograph records could also be counted on to have a market for more than a hundred thousand piano rolls. Berlin, Leo Feist, and officers of the other companies were charged with violating the Sherman Anti-Trust Act. Among the nine companies, they controlled eighty percent of America's music output of records, sheet music, and piano rolls. The government charged that they had not only fixed prices but had refused to deal with any manufacturer who didn't keep to their stipulations. The music men were ordered finally to dissolve the Consolidated Music Corporation which they had set up among them to fix and maintain prices. It was a blow, but not one which had much effect on Berlin's life.

He was, however, going to have to recover from a personal blow which fate had inevitably dealt him: Leah Baline died. In a Brooklyn cemetery, her Izzy recited Kaddish, the memorial prayer he had been taught as an eight-year-old when his father died.

8

A Pretty Girl Is Like a Melody

IF MOSES BALINE COULD have seen the way his son was now able to live, if he had been told the size of his son's fortune, he would have believed neither his eyes nor his ears. Such things, to Moses, could have been true only of the Tsar and his palace.

From Berlin's point of view, he was making a very nice living indeed. But the tensions of hard work seemed not to have diminished any since he had first experienced the thrill of being warmly welcomed by his bank manager. His best work still came at night; insomnia had become a pattern. And, as he said, the most difficult thing of all was trying to live up to his own reputation.

Reporters asked him repeatedly what his method was for creating a good song, just as if, for their readers' sakes, they were going to a broker for tips on the stock market.

Throwing his hat on the table in front of him, Berlin once pondered the question and came up with this answer, "Usually, a phrase hits me first. I keep repeating it over and over, and the first thing I know, I begin to get a sort of rhythm. Then a tune. Not all my songs are written that way. Sometimes I hear a tune first and then start trying to fit words to it. In either case, whichever part comes first serves as a mold into which the other part must be poured."

Florenz Ziegfeld had successfully courted Berlin into writing shows. Now, in 1921, Irving Berlin was courting himself. He wanted his own theater, not just his own publishing company. He wanted to be able to hear people applauding his music inside his own palace.

The notion had taken root after a discussion with Sam H. Harris, a legendary Broadway figure with experience in running a show business empire. For years he had been George M. Cohan's partner. One day Harris told Berlin he wanted his own theater.

The idea was forgotten until the two happened to come together again. "Sam," Berlin announced, "I have a name for that theater of yours. Why not call it The Music Box?"

Harris liked the name so much he changed his mind about ownership and suggested that Berlin be partner. "Then we could call it," he said, "Irving Berlin's Music Box."

Berlin turned down the name. "That would be too much Berlin," he said. But he accepted the offer of partnership.

The theater, to be built on Forty-fifth Street, was going to be the most ornate playhouse of its kind with the plushest seats and the deepest carpets. As Broadway habitués suggested, it was going to reek with class. As the building went up, there was more and more evidence of the money being sunk into it, and there was always talk at the Friars Club or the Lambs of some new extravagance.

"I guess the boys are building themselves a monument," began one exchange.

"A monument?" countered his friend. "More likely a tombstone."

Costs rose astronomically for the show Berlin was writing as The Music Box opener. With every dab of gold paint added to the theater's walls, Berlin was closer to reaching the end of his available cash.

Joseph Schenck, soon to become studio boss of United Artists in Hollywood, came to Berlin's aid. At the time Berlin was a singing waiter, Schenck had been clerking in a Bowery drugstore.

Berlin told Schenck: "I'm in trouble." To which Schenck replied: "Okay. Who is she?"

"It's not a girl," Berlin replied. "It's a theater."

Schenck put up half the extra money Berlin needed to invest and became his partner, with Berlin promising to buy him out the moment he could afford to. And so they went ahead—Harris supervising the building arrangements, Berlin getting his show together. He confessed to particular enjoyment of one part of the job, interviewing the chorus girls. But what really delighted him was to have written a tune for his new theater which pleased him more than anything he had ever written before. Its name, he thought, would live after him: "Say It with Music." The show itself was to be called simply *The Music Box Revue.*

Sam Harris was excited by everything about it. Allowing himself an entrepreneur's fancy, he wrote and sent out a press release, on his own letterhead, which read:

The young man who has puckered the lips of a nation into a whistling position, stimulated the hurdy-gurdy industry and increased the dividends of the gramophone and pianola companies is going on the stage.

This does not mean that Mr. Berlin has written his last song. It simply means that he will have to get up a little earlier every day despite his predilection to slumber.

Sam H. Harris announces that Mr. Berlin will be a member of the company opening in *The Music Box Revue*. Mr. Berlin's present working day averages about twelve hours. And I felt that time was hanging heavily on his hands. Accordingly, I offered him a job. I believe that everyone should work. Besides, he is a fine young fellow and I want to see him get ahead. When I expressed my feelings, he took the job.

At the bottom of the press release was a little announcement that The Music Box had cost over one million dollars before show expenses were taken into consideration.

The Music Box Revue opened on September 22, 1921, even more Berlin's show than the Follies were Ziegfeld's. He was billed above the title, he wrote all the music, appeared in sketches, played the piano, and sang a tune or two.

The theatre was magnificent. The show kept the audience mesmerized. One critic wrote, "The Music Box was opened last evening before a palpitant audience and proved to be a treasure chest out of which the conjurers pulled all manner of gay tunes and brilliant trappings and funny clowns and nimble dancers. Its contents confirmed the dark suspicion that Sam H. Harris and Irving Berlin have gone quite mad. The sumptuous and be-spangled revue cannot possibly earn them anything more substantial than the heartwarming satisfaction of having produced it all."

The critic was right about the satisfaction, wrong about the earnings. Soon there was enough cash coming into the box office to allow Berlin to pay Schenck back the money he had borrowed.

Berlin went on writing other songs, including the classic "All by Myself," and began planning *The Second Music Box Revue.* He was feeling very confident, not just for himself, but for American music in general. He told a reporter, "In the next two years, American syncopation will so influence the classical music of the world that New York will be getting operas from Vienna filled to the brim with our own native jazz."

People fell on his every word, despite such exaggerated judgments and he was often interviewed by the press. Berlin was always scrupulously polite to callers. He would look intently at the interviewer, his legs crossed, hands clasped. Only the telephone could interrupt him.

One day a call informed him that a water leak had developed in the theatre. It wasn't major, but no one could find the cause. Only after professional study was the source revealed. The theatre had been built over an old, long-forgotten natural spring. No one, even builders, ever thought of Broadway in terms of its original terrain.

Just as the 1922 *Music Box Revue* was about to get underway, Berlin paid a return visit to the Bowery for "Nigger" Mike's funeral. "He was no angel, maybe," he commented when he got back. "But there are a lot of guys on the street today who would have been in jail if it hadn't been for Mike."

Bobby Clark and Paul McCullough were in the cast of the new show, as were the Fairbanks Twins. The songs were not as memorable as they had been in the first edition, but people enjoyed numbers like "Crinoline Days," "Lady of the Evening," and the Ziegfeldesque "My Diamond Horseshoe of Girls."

Berlin's routine was to spend his afternoons in the theatre, play poker for astonishingly high stakes in the evening, and then stay up with his piano. When things were going well, he was a joy to know. When things were difficult for him, or when his insomnia produced no creativity, he was slightly less amiable.

One thing that *never* pleased him was an arrangement of a Berlin song that owed more to the arranger than to the composer. If, as sometimes happened, a publisher sent him a record with an unusual arrangement of a Berlin song, particularly one he did not like, he would get so incensed that he would all but break the disk on his knee. Nine times out of ten, the offending publisher heard from Berlin's lawyers in the morning.

The Roaring Twenties had begun, but Berlin took time out from the spirit of the decade to wax patriotic with "Three Cheers for the Red, White and Blue."

In 1923, humorist Robert Benchley made his first stage appearance in *The Fourth Music Box Revue.* "Nothing could be more discouraging than a rehearsal shortly preceding the opening of the Music Box," he wrote to Alexander Woollcott. "Out there are perhaps a dozen men with their hats on, each sitting on as much of an aisle seat as he can uncover from the big sheet which spreads out over all the orchestra chairs. The house is dark except for what crazy lights come up from the stage. The director climbs up on the stage with the stage managers. 'All right, now. Music, please. All right, tiger skin girls!'

"The pianist plays several bars and is stopped again. Then a little man in a tight-fitting suit with his hands in his pockets walks on from the wings. He looks very white in the glare from the foots.

You almost expect him to be thrown out, he seems so casual and like an observer. They don't throw him out, however, because he is Mr. Berlin.

"You are suddenly overcome with a feeling of tremendous futility. 'Irving Berlin's Fourth Music Box Revue' it already says in lights out in front of the theater. Irving Berlin is so little. And *The Fourth Music Box Revue* is so big."

What surprised Benchley, he told Woollcott (who subsequently published the letter in his short "Story of Irving Berlin" in 1924) was that a man could work night and day for four months as Berlin had done getting this show ready, engaging principals as well as writing all the words and music, and in that time no one heard him raise his voice and no one was hurt by him.

"Now you know," he concluded, "why you can't get it all from the front on opening night, all of The Music Box or all of Irving Berlin."

Looking at the phenomenon that was Irving Berlin that year, John Alden Carpenter, a composer of more serious music, decided, "I am strongly inclined to believe that the musical historian of the year 2000 will find the birthday of American music and that of Irving Berlin to have been the same." Woollcott, however, called Berlin "a creative ignoramus."

Had Berlin been able to read and play music properly, he might or might not have been a brilliant musician. But by 1924, what he dictated to his musical secretary came from a mind with gifts that no lessons or practice could have inspired.

"It was," he told the *New York Times*, "no more than being able to recognize what rhythm meant, and being with the times. It was the age of the automobile," he said. "The speed and snap of American jazz music is influenced by the automobile's popularity. Wagner, Beethoven, Mendelssohn, Liszt. All the masters of music knew the value of movement. Crashing out to us come the songs of triumphant armies, or perhaps the changing notes tell of twilight with lovers dancing on the village green. All these sounds speak of action.

"The automobile, however, is a new method of movement. All the old rhythm is gone and in its place is heard the hum of an engine, the whirr of wheels, the explosion of an exhaust. The leisurely songs that men hummed to the clatter of horses' hoofs do not fit into this new rhythm. The new age demands new music for new action.

"I have been told that 'Alexander's Ragtime Band' was the first notable piece of syncopation. With all due modesty, I think I can say that I was the first to write a popular song that was a decided change from the conventional music of that time. Syncopation allows for broken harmonies, 'ragged time' as the musicians first called it."

The automobile theme was one he seemed to like. In another *Times* interview he said, "The jazz composers have not really begun to write. Jazz is today where the automobile was in 1899. There is a profound and lasting quality in American popular music that assures it of constant development.

"When I say that jazz is the only great contribution of the 20th century to the music annals of the world, I am speaking with the utmost seriousness. It is young, and being young, it has its faults. But none that can't be corrected. It will thrive because there is nothing artificial about it. Its tremendous popularity is due to the fact that it sounds a note to which millions of Americans are responsive."

He repeated an ambition. "The jazz opera will be a natural development. I hope that some day I may write an operatic score in jazz."

Despite public acclaim, despite financial success, it threatened his security to feel that he was just a "creative ignoramus." Defensively, to ward off someone else's calling attention to it, Berlin constantly referred to his lack of formal training. The idea of the opera was probably reserved as some kind of final proving ground.

The question of "what the public wants" was the subject of a collective discourse presented for readers of the *New York Times*

Sunday Magazine in March 1924. The entertainment wizards being asked were: David W. Griffith, David Belasco, George M. Cohan, Harry Lauder, producer Morris Gest, short-story writer Fannie Hurst, and, of course, Irving Berlin.

"The public wants anything that is good," was the gist of his remarks, "and the only way to learn if it *is* good is to try it on them."

Paul Whiteman's band had become one of the big bands of the day where Berlin peddled his tunes in person. "You've never played one like this before," he'd tell Whiteman, who had a new young singer named Bing Crosby. Berlin's black eyes glistened with every sale.

But radio had come on the scene and brought with it a fact that was going to haunt him for years to come. If people can hear tunes on the radio they are not going to be so ready to buy music to play at home. And even if they do hear it and buy it too, they are going to become tired of it a lot more quickly than before. Which might be good for business at first. But would the public go on forking out cash for music they could hear somewhere else for nothing? And just what would the composer's position be in the matter of copyright?

Berlin persuaded twenty-four other songwriters—including Victor Herbert, John Philip Sousa, Harry von Tilzer, and Charles K. Harris—to go with him to Washington and state their case before the Senate Patents Committee. They demanded the right to royalties every time radio stations broadcast their tunes.

While in Washington, the twenty-five put on a show for the National Press Club. Berlin thumped on the black notes and produced a recognizable rendering of his new Music Box hit, "Lazy." He sang it too, and 300 assembled pressmen were plainly delighted. They demanded more. "Alexander's Ragtime Band," called one. And the composer obliged. "Play 'That Mesmerizing Mendelssohn Tune,' " called another with a long memory, and Berlin was able to produce that, too.

It was a presidential election year and the Democrats were determined to wrest power from the Republicans and Calvin Coolidge. "Keep Cool with Coolidge" was the campaign song the Republicans whistled, hummed, and sang whenever there was a gathering large enough to appreciate it. When Al Jolson sang the song for them, they were sure to draw an even larger audience.

The Democrats called on Irving Berlin to provide an anthem for Governor Al Smith of New York. He needed something inspiring. As a Catholic, he was a gamble whichever way one looked at it. It was up to Irving Berlin to lift both the Governor's spirits and his chances at the polls. Smith had already adopted "The Sidewalks of New York" as his own personal theme tune. It was played every time he led a parade and it seemed that in New York, the Governor was always leading parades. The song became so much a part of Smith's style, in fact, that people believed he had written it himself.

So when Berlin took on the job of writing a new campaign song, it was clear it had to have some relation to the old one. He chose to adapt the familiar melody and provide a new set of lyrics, with the title, "We'll All Go Voting for Al."

For the duration of the campaign, the new song *did* seem to be the successor to "The Sidewalks of New York," but after Smith moved into the Governor's mansion, both he and his constituents went back to singing the old song.

Important people fascinated Berlin—especially as subjects for songs. The year before he wrote Al Smith's campaign song, he had written a number that was never published, called "His Royal Shyness," in honor of the Prince of Wales, who had just made a sensationally successful tour of the United States.

The Prince, feted wherever he went, had been a guest at the Long Island home of Clarence Mackay, head of the American Posts and Telegraph Company. While there, the Prince had danced with Mackay's daughter, Ellin.

"She is one of the most charming girls I have ever met," the Prince was heard to remark, and the fact was duly transmitted along the society grapevine. Tongues wagged wherever the Prince went, and every time he had a girl to dance with the rumors of a possible new royal romance flew.

When Irving Berlin was seen to dance with Ellin Mackay at a party, the couple was immediately linked together by the gossip. After all, he had danced with the girl who had danced with the Prince of Wales.

9

The Girl That I Marry

IT WAS A STORY that had all the elements of a fairy tale—a charming prince, a beautiful girl, and a once-poor boy. The rumors were extravagant. The facts were quite enough to satisfy anyone's craving for romance.

Berlin had met Ellin Mackay at about the time she met the Prince. (One story had it that Edward acted as a go-between for them, engaging Ellin's father in long conversations so that she could make secret telephone calls to Berlin, the man she loved.) The actual introduction, at any rate, was at a party given by a young artist. From there Ellin and Berlin had gone on to dance the hours away at a nightclub. As dawn broke, Ellin drove him home in her own rakish red roadster. From then on, they were seen at a number of parties together, including one at Harbor Hill, the Roslyn, Long Island home of Clarence Mackay.

Mackay was the multi-millionaire son of an Irish-Scots immigrant whose name was pronounced "Mackey." His father John had made a fortune from the great gold and silver bonanza in Nevada. John had wooed his wife, a young widow, with the words, "I'll give you the world on a silver platter." And he did. Owner of the Comstock Lode silver mines, he saw shares of his company rise overnight in 1872 from fifteen cents to $1,850 each.

His son Clarence was wealthy, snobbish, Catholic, and anti-Semitic. The Mackay house on Long Island, which stood on a

73

thousand acres of land, was like a French chateau. There were magnificent paintings and tapestries, precious collections of everything from china to suits of armor.

Part of John Mackay's mining fortune had been invested in the infant telegraph system. Clarence now owned the Mackay-Bennett Ocean Cable, which later became the Commercial Telegraph Company, and also the Postal Telegraph Company. Divorced, Mackay liked to spend time duck shooting or sailing on one of his steam yachts. Under any circumstances, Irving Berlin would not have been his sort of fellow. As a suitor for his daughter, he was entirely unacceptable.

When it was apparent that Ellin and Berlin were seeing rather too much of each other, Mackay decided to put brakes on the affair. Ellin was barely twenty when Clarence, known to newspapermen as the "Cable King," took her abroad in 1924 to get her away from Berlin. Spain, France, Britain, Italy—in Rome they had an audience with the Pope—and then to Egypt and Algiers. Their Vatican visit inspired rumors in the U.S. that Ellin had gone to ask for a dispensation to allow her to marry Berlin.

The Mackays' absence did not cool Berlin's ardor nor the gossip mongers' interest. His big hit of the year was "All Alone," and the story went that it was an expression of Berlin's feelings at being away from Ellin. But he denied it to the press with cold detachment. People said the same thing about "What'll I Do?" which was sung over the radio in the first of countless broadcast tributes to Irving Berlin, and he denied that, too.

In London, he wrote "Remember," and people who thought they knew said that it had most certainly been inspired by his now floundering love affair. But he denied that as well.

"The idea is ridiculous," he was reported saying. "Just because a man writes sob ballads, he is not writing from his own experiences. . . . The real reason is that right now the public would rather buy tears than smiles. They happen to want sob ballads. The only song I ever wrote out of my own personal experience was 'When I Lost You' when my wife died."

Ellin returned to America after seven months. Both she and her father denied rumors of romance or an impending engagement. Ellin was going to spend the next few years writing books and magazine articles.

"The truth of the matter is," she said when the S.S. *Olympic* docked, "that if I were to marry I would have to surrender the companionship of my father, and I can't bear to think of parting with Dad.

"How could that rumor of an engagement ever have been started?" she asked the battery of reporters waiting for her. "It's natural that after a girl has made her debut, people expect her to marry. But I have not met the young man I would marry to give up my father. If you print any story of my engagement, I will simply have to deny it later to my friends."

Pressed further, she went on. "It is true that I have met Mr. Berlin at parties, but I have met many men at social events and I don't see that this calls for the creation of something out of nothing. I am not engaged to anyone."

Asked if she would marry a man who wasn't wealthy, she fired back, "Are you proposing?" And she drove off to Harbor Hill assuming that the bluff had worked. It hadn't.

Reporters went straight from the dock to Berlin's apartment at twenty-nine West Forty-sixth Street, and then invaded his Broadway offices.

"I am not engaged to anyone," he told them. "Except to Sam Harris. And I'm engaged to write two new shows for him—one for the Marx Brothers and one for the Music Box Revue."

Berlin felt uncomfortable about the publicity. Ellin was rather amused by it. But her father seethed.

Clarence Mackay contacted his lawyers immediately after reading the newspapers and issued a statement. "My attention has been drawn," he said, as though referring to the complaints of his stockholders, "to an article this day published in a morning paper. It contained so many false statements that to treat any of them in detail would serve no useful purpose. There are, therein, three statements of very grave import, not merely to me but to others and perhaps even to a substantial part of the community and these I wish to meet with a denial of the strongest character.

"1) His Holiness the Pope has never sanctioned and has never been asked to sanction a marriage between a daughter of mine and the person referred to."

"2) I have not sought nor held an interview with that gentleman, nor have I ever seen him."

"3) I know of no engagement between my daughter and him."

When Berlin was shown the statement, he commented, "Quite right. I don't know where the story came from."

Then he promptly phoned Ellin to tell her how much he loved and wanted to marry her.

Photographs of both of them appeared frequently in the newspapers, but they never were shown together. They were always careful to see that they weren't spotted with each other.

Stories about their private lives were rife. "Mr. Berlin," according to one paper's scoop, "lives on boiled eggs and once called the Queen of England a peach."

The romance had so caught the public imagination that a pair of rival songwriters, Jimmy McHugh and Al Dublin, rhapsodized about them in a song they called "When a Kid Who Came from the East Side Found a Sweet Society Rose." Berlin himself was working on the Marx Brothers show *Coconuts,* and suing an amusement park owner for playing a Berlin number without his consent.

Other girls tried to get their names linked with Berlin's just as hard as Ellin tried to keep hers from being coupled with his. Arriving in Boston once to attend the theater, Berlin was asked if it were true that he had taken an interest in a Mrs. Leonard Rhinelander.

She was formerly Alice Jones, a housemaid, and now Rhinelander was suing to have their marriage annulled. She produced in court letters that showed "she was one of the most sought-after girls in the world. Al Jolson had noticed her and so had Irving Berlin." Berlin had never laid eyes on the lady.

He was, however, in touch with Clarence Mackay, and the discussion that resulted was a heated one.

"The day you marry my daughter, I'll disinherit her," one report says Mackay fumed.

"The day I marry your daughter," the suitor replied, "I'll settle two million dollars on her."

Columnists gave free rein to their imaginations in reporting the confrontation. One story had Mackay telling Berlin that his family had a proud pedigree. "So have I," Berlin was supposed to have countered. "I can trace mine back to the Exodus."

"In that case," replied Mackay in the stories, "you're now faced with another Exodus. Get out."

Despite the exaggeration, it had been a flaming session. Soon afterward Berlin told someone, "I'm worth more than four million dollars and that's enough for Clarence Mackay's daughter, or any other woman, to live on." For the record, though, he was still denying any romance.

Meanwhile, Ellin had made her avowed excursion into journalism. An article of hers was published in *The New Yorker*. In it, she deplored the fact that since people of all classes were now invited to social functions, society girls had to seek refuge in cabarets. "In cabarets, at least we do not have to dance with them," she wrote. Her father would have been pleased with that sentiment.

Her father, in fact, may have been too apoplectic that week to turn the pages of any magazine. He had just learned, as the magazine hit the stands, that his daughter had eloped. With the person referred to.

January 4, 1926, was the day that James J. Walker had settled in for the first time at City Hall as Mayor of New York. That day the Queen of Italy died, and the Prince of Wales captured a runaway horse. All these news items vied for space on front pages the next day with the story that Ellin Mackay and Irving Berlin had married.

At six o'clock the previous morning Benny Bloom, Berlin's publicity manager, had had a telephone call. "Get over here by eleven, Benny. We have to be down at the Municipal Building at noon."

Max Winslow, a partner in Irving Berlin Inc., had a similar call to come over, "and bring Tillie with you." "I knew something was up," Winslow said later, "because he doesn't usually get out of bed till two in the afternoon."

He and his wife Tillie, together with Benny Bloom, came to Berlin's apartment. They would be witnesses at the wedding. Ellin was already there. Berlin had phoned her too, and it was only then that they decided to get married. She got her car out of the garage at the Mackay townhouse on East Seventy-fifth Street and drove down to Forty-sixth.

"Listen, we've gotta get down to the Municipal Building right away," Winslow told them. "There are a lot of things to get done."

Driving down to the Municipal Building meant the chance they would be spotted and mobbed at a traffic stop. So it became a notable day indeed for Ellin. It was her first subway ride.

They arrived at the Municipal Building just as Deputy City Clerk James J. McCormick was going off to lunch.

"That's Irving Berlin," a startled clerk shouted to McCormick. He stopped and shook Berlin's hand warmly, then went on to greet Ellin and the Winslows.

"So you're getting married today and Mr. Berlin's going to be your witness?" he asked Winslow, who then had to explain to the official that he was already married and that Berlin, not he, was taking a bride. McCormick was one man who did not read newspapers.

Meanwhile Benny Bloom had collected the necessary marriage license forms. With Berlin dictating the details, Bloom filled them all out. Born: Russia. Mother's maiden name: Leah

Lipkin. Father's name: Moses Baline. Then it was Ellin's turn. Her name was originally spelled Ell*e*n, she said, so that was how it appeared on the license. Her mother's maiden name was Katherine Duer. Her father? On Ellin's instructions, that line was left blank. If he were going to disinherit her, she was at least going to disown him.

"Let's get on with it then," said McCormick.

Both bride and groom wore gray suits for the ceremony. Ellin had an orange cloche over her fashionably bobbed hair. She clearly enjoyed every moment of the ceremony. He was just as clearly a bundle of nerves.

After the kissing and handshaking, all five made for telephone booths to let close friends know of the wedding. No one put through a call to Harbor House.

One of Ellin's calls was to Harold Ross, editor of *The New Yorker*. "Hello, Miss Mackay," Ross said when she was put through to him.

"Oh, no," she told him. "It's Mrs. Berlin now. The fact is . . . I won't be able to get my piece in on time. I'm leaving town soon."

The news was not long in reaching people who hadn't been phoned direct. Clarence Mackay was informed during a business conference in his New York offices. He promptly issued another statement to the press and left for home. His statement was right to the point. "The marriage has been performed without my knowledge or approval," and that was all he intended to say about the matter.

Ellin's mother, now happily married to society surgeon Dr. Joseph Blake, was also keeping tight-lipped: "I have nothing to say one way or the other." Friends thought it was more a case of Mrs. Blake's being denied the pleasure of being present at her daughter's wedding than pique at her marrying a Jewish songwriter. The *New York Times* commented, "In fact some quarters pictured her as desirous of seeing her daughter follow the dictates of her own heart."

At four o'clock that afternoon, the Berlins went downstairs

and faced the horde of reporters. Yes, they were married; no, they had not heard from Mr. Mackay. Fighting their way through the crowd, they got in Berlin's coupe. There they sat. They couldn't do much else. Ellin had phoned her maid and asked her to bring down some things so that the couple could leave on a short honeymoon, but the maid hadn't turned up.

Reporters pressed their faces to the car window. Berlin rolled one down briefly. "We were married and we are very happy," he told the faces. "That's all we care to say."

The newlyweds stared into space. Ellin glanced back through the rear window occasionally and looked at her watch. They were planning to pay a call on her mother and then they had a train to Atlantic City to catch, but they were going to miss it if the maid didn't come soon. To closed windows the reporters read aloud Clarence Mackay's statement, but the couple appeared unmoved.

The maid and a suitcase of Ellin's clothes finally arrived, and the couple drove off.

Newsmen had taken bets on Florida or an Adirondack resort honeymoon. Others thought the whole departure thing had been a ruse and that they were staying in town. Yet most of them felt that someone like Irving Berlin wouldn't be satisfied with just an East Coast honeymoon, especially when only a couple of days earlier he had cancelled a reservation to sail for Europe on the White Star liner *Homeric*.

It turned out that a lot of the guessing had been right. They were back in town that night after missing the train. And they were going to Europe five days later, sailing in a five-thousand-dollar suite on the *Leviathan*, along with at least a dozen movie stars and one of the Shubert brothers.

That first evening at the Berlin apartment, Irving and Ellin had dinner with the Winslows and then drove off unnoticed for Atlantic City. This time there was a chauffeur. In the early hours of January 5, they booked into the Ritz Carlton Hotel and were shown to an ocean-view suite. They didn't register. The hotel agreed it might help them escape notice.

After a late breakfast, they went for a stroll along the famous Boardwalk and slipped back in time for lunch in their suite. But at three o'clock, on their way out for another walk, their luck left them as they were spotted in the hotel lobby.

"It's Irving Berlin and Ellin," shrilled one guest, and then they were mobbed.

"Congratulations," people shouted. "Good luck!"

One man forced his way through the crowd, kissed Ellin on the cheek, and pumped Irving's hand. It was W. K. Vanderbilt, Jr., a close friend of Ellin's father, who was nonetheless delighted that love had triumphed. Ellin glowed as she accepted the good wishes showered on them, and Irving just stood smiling at the fuss that was being made. Ellin had apparently persuaded him to enjoy it. He even laughed when a man in the crowd made the sort of remark that bridegrooms are braced to expect.

Then came the reporters. "The only thing I want to say," Ellin teased them, "is that I hope I will *never* be seen wearing a red coat and an orange hat as one of you reported recently." That remark seemed to win over the press. "You do the talking, dear," Irving said.

"We're very anxious for my father to give his consent and blessing," she went on.

"Nothing to say, Mr. Berlin?"

"We're hoping it will be granted," he allowed.

"The report is not true," Ellin said next, "that my father telegraphed me a warning not to seek his forgiveness. I haven't heard from Father at all. Of course I hope he will forgive me. But we're supremely happy and that's what counts."

Berlin spoke up. "Don't think all this happened overnight," he said. "This is no publicity stunt. We're in love."

"Oh, yes," said Ellin, "we've known each other for years." What she said next gladdened the heart of every woman reporter present.

"Actually, I got married in my very oldest dress. I didn't have time to change because we were married so soon after we made up our minds to go through with it. Before he called me yesterday morning, I had no idea of being married so soon. He just said, 'Ellin, I want you to decide now one way or the other.' So I decided. I love him and he loves me, so I'm confident I took the right step."

Ellin was asked if she would continue her career as a writer. She laughed. "Well, I've got Irving to support me now. I suppose I won't really *have* to write." That was good for another appreciative chuckle from reporters.

Then it was time to pose for pictures. Other reporters went scurrying for any new angle or sidelight they could turn up. One of them found Mrs. A. B. Kahn, Berlin's sister, supervising the newspaper delivery rounds for a stationer in Montclair, New Jersey.

Berlin's success hadn't altered her life very much. Her husband ran a newspaper delivery service from a shop on Bloomfield Avenue. "I can't understand all the interest in the wedding," Mrs. Kahn said. "I've been expecting Izzy to marry for a year."

Ellin was sure that her father would finally sanction the match. On the third day of being Mrs. Berlin, she phoned Mackay but was told he wouldn't speak to her. She and Irving left the Ritz Carlton two days earlier than expected. As she walked to the car, she was biting her lip and had a handkerchief at her eyes. They drove straight back to New York.

Berlin's butler Ivan was instructed to tell reporters that they were staying the night and that there would be no statement. It was now very much what reporters called a running story; Forty-sixth Street was their stake-out. Would the couple stay in New York for the forthcoming society wedding of Consuelo Vanderbilt and E. T. Smith?

Within twenty-four hours the Berlins were back in Atlantic City, Ellin's tears dried. She had organized a party for sixty at the Ritz Carlton that night.

"It's mostly for my friends," she said as guests arrived at the hotel's ballroom. "I want you to meet my husband."

One invited guest didn't accept. She had sent a special delivery letter to Clarence Mackay, but he had not even opened it.

Reporters, of course, tried to crash the party, but the Berlins knew the guest list. "No statement, I said," Berlin told them angrily. Would they at least pose for pictures? They did.

Straight after the party, the couple left for the station on their way back to New York. Again they were mobbed. Again it was the same chatter. "It's the Berlins." "There's Ellin." "Has her father forgiven her yet?"

As soon as the gate to the platform opened, they stepped through and entered their own private car. Ellin sank into her seat and began crying again. "Will there now be a religious ceremony?" someone asked her, pressing his way into the compartment.

Berlin answered for her. "It's too early to talk about ceremonies. We can't say anything now."

"Mrs. Berlin, have you heard from Mr. Mackay?"

"I'm sorry to say I haven't," said Ellin, her emotions again in control. "I'm disappointed that Father hasn't come to see us. We're supremely happy," she said, again using her favorite phrase. "But I'm also heartsick." She bit her handkerchief nervously. Newspaper readers were getting a real-life novelette for the price of two cents.

Berlin was all politeness. "Well, boys, you'll have to excuse us now," he said, ushering them out of the car. But most of the reporters stayed with them on the train. Berlin popped his head out of their private compartment only once during the journey: "Just say we're tickled to death with married life." If they could survive the press, the next fifty years or so would be nothing to worry about.

They left the train at Newark, New Jersey, where the chauffeur was waiting for them. He managed to get them home in time to run to the front door before photographers had a chance to catch them. But crowds gathered in the lobby of the apartment building and were not easily put off. Despite the fact that the chauffeur made it obvious that he had delivered the last suitcase and had driven the Berlin car to the garage, they stayed hour after hour.

Next day Clarence Mackay's lawyer said he knew nothing of the rumors that his client had filed a new will, disinheriting Ellin completely. It was generally agreed that he had, but no details were forthcoming.

The Berlins were now in a state of siege. They did not turn up at the Vanderbilt wedding, nor did they go anywhere else. Since they were newlyweds, it didn't really matter to them. Berlin had a special wedding present ready for Ellin. As she unwrapped the sheet of music, she saw the title—"Always." Its first line . . . "I'll be loving you—always."

It was more than just sentiment. The song would have had value had the romance died that moment. Berlin had arranged with his lawyer to assign the copyright and all royalties over to Ellin. Twenty years later, she had made more than half a million dollars from the gift.

The romance, of course, did not die. It was obvious that they were every bit as "supremely happy" as Ellin had claimed.

Berlin himself told me, " 'Always' was a love song I wrote because I had fallen in love."

He had planned originally to have "Always" incorporated into the score of *Coconuts*, but George S. Kaufman, who wrote the book, didn't like it.

The two men had adjoining suites in a hotel so they could work separately but closely on the show for about two weeks. At five o'clock one morning, Berlin rushed into Kaufman's room, shook him awake and said, "George, I've got something new for you to hear. Tell me what you think. . . ." He shouldn't have done it. At any hour of the day Kaufman didn't have much of an ear for music.

"Irving has a pure but hardly strong voice," Kaufman said

years later. "And since I am not very strong myself at five o'clock in the morning, I could not catch a word of it."

But Berlin sat on the edge of Kaufman's bed and sang it again. He had to hum it three times before it got through. Kaufman said he didn't like the words that much. It seemed to him ridiculous that anyone would commit himself to loving anyone else for "always." "Try 'I'll be loving you on Thursday,'" suggested his collaborator. Berlin was not amused.

On the January night in 1926 that Berlin presented Ellin with "Always," their apartment was flooded with telegrams from reporters desperate for a new statement. Berlin answered each with a telegram of his own.

WE DESIRE TO AVOID PUBLICITY BUT WE HAVE BEEN MISQUOTED SO MUCH THAT WE WISH TO MAKE THIS STATEMENT IN ORDER TO SET TO REST THE FABRICATIONS THAT HAVE BEEN PUBLISHED IN CERTAIN NEWSPAPERS STOP.

WE HAVE NEVER SAID ONE WORD FOR PUBLICATION EXCEPT THAT WE ARE VERY HAPPY STOP THAT STATEMENT WE REPEAT AND BEYOND THAT WE HAVE NOTHING TO SAY STOP.

On January 8, the *Leviathan* sailed for Europe with the Berlins on board. The Associated Press immediately telegraphed Clarence Mackay for a statement. A telegram came in return from William J. Deegan, Vice President of the Mackay Corporations.

MR. MACKAY HAS ASKED ME TO EXPRESS HIS THANKS FOR YOUR VERY COURTEOUS TELEGRAM AND IN REPLY REQUESTS ME TO SAY THAT HE SEES NO REASON FOR MAKING ANY STATEMENT OTHER THAN THE ONE HE ISSUED ON MONDAY LAST AND WHICH IS THE ONLY STATEMENT WITH REGARD TO THE MATTER WHICH HE ISSUED AND AUTHORIZED STOP THE MARRIAGE CAME AS A COMPLETE SURPRISE TO ME AND WAS DONE WITHOUT MY KNOWLEDGE AND APPROVAL STOP BEYOND THAT I HAVE NOTHING TO SAY STOP STATEMENTS PUBLISHED SINCE WERE FALSE STOP.

Meanwhile, *Vogue* magazine's latest edition had come out. In it, an article by Ellin Mackay discussed Mondays at the Opera, college football games, and her feelings (spiteful) about debutantes. As for fashion, she thought old styles were coming back.

The Berlins' cabin on "C" deck of the *Leviathan,* especially designed for the Kaiser, was now known as the Presidential Suite. Rudolph Valentino, Mary Pickford, and Douglas Fairbanks had traveled in it. Special arrangements for this trip had included a piano in the suite for Berlin.

The ship's captain, rather indiscreetly for one who is expected to exercise diplomacy, radioed home, "I've often traveled with honeymooners, but rarely have I been kept busier than by these. They spent a small fortune replying to scores of radiograms." Then he added, "None of them have come from the bride's father."

In mid-Atlantic they played deck games. In the evenings they danced in the first-class ballroom, often to Berlin tunes like "All Alone" and "Remember."

"Are you writing a new love song on the ship?" asked a fellow passenger on the dance floor. "No, I'm leaving work alone for a while," was the answer.

"How about a bridal march in ragtime?" someone else called. "No. Not this time," he said, and went on dancing.

Each day, a new bouquet of roses, ordered for them by phone from friends in New York, was brought to the honeymooners' cabin.

While they were away, a report appeared that a religious ceremony had been arranged for at St. Patrick's Cathedral. The same day, another report stressed that Berlin would continue to be a Jew (he had donated a thousand dollars to the United Jewish Campaign), while Ellin had no desire to give up Catholicism.

In February, the *Social Register* of New York "recorded" the marriage with this curt information: "Miss Ellin Mackay, daughter of Clarence Mackay, and Mr. Irving Berlin were married on January 4 in New York." The *Register* was quick to point out: "This is in accordance with the *Social Register*'s custom of recording marriages when one of the parties is in Society."

The *New York Times* was equally quick to point out that the announcement was not made in the *Social Register*'s usual style of "Mr. and Mrs. Irving Berlin." It also noted that there was no guarantee that either name would ever appear in the *Register* again. Neither ever did.

10

I'll Be Loving You—Always

WHETHER HE LIKED IT or not, Berlin's whirlwind romance had made his life public property on both sides of the Atlantic. Long before the *Leviathan* approached the shores of Southampton, his London manager, Joshua Low, had the British press on his hands. Was there any truth to the rumor that Ellin wasn't really on board with Irving? That he had left her in New York and come to London strictly on business? No, she was on board with him. And no, he had not made it up with his father-in-law.

Echoing the question of the ballroom dancer on board, someone asked why Berlin hadn't written a bridal march.

"For the simple reason that there is no money in bridal marches," said Low. By being so direct, he hoped reporters would be sympathetic. "Tell your readers," Low went on, "what a nice fellow Irving is. You might care to mention how reasonable he is about the price of his songs. But he won't tell you anything about his marriage."

The couple arrived at London's Waterloo Station to what the *Daily Express* described as "an astonishing reception." Just how astonishing became apparent soon after the Berlins stepped from the train and walked down the platform with an escort of porters. As they got halfway down the crowded platform, shielded from the other passengers by a galaxy of railway staff, forty men gathered in a group around them and began singing:

"Drink! Drink! Let the toast start! Drink! Drink! May your hearts nev-er part. Let ev-er-y lover sa-lute his sweet-heart."

The Berlins stood rooted, baffled. Then one of the singers stepped forward and approached them. "Mr. . . . err . . . Shubert?" he stammered.

"Shubert?" asked Berlin with dawning awareness and annoyance.

"No, no, this is Irving Berlin," said one of the porters, jumping in to keep an embarrassing moment from becoming more so.

"My God," said the singer, "we thought he was Jake Shubert!"

"Well who are *you* people then?" asked the railwayman, warming to a joke that was funny only to those outside the muddle. "We're the chorus from *The Student Prince,* and we came here to welcome Mr. Schubert, the theater man from New York."

Mr. Shubert, it turned out, had not come directly to London as planned, but had left the *Leviathan* at Cherbourg and gone on to Paris to buy costumes for his next Broadway production.

Once they realized what had happened, the chorus grouped themselves again and we went on to sing other *Student Prince* numbers. Though Berlin felt they were advertising a rival production on his own time, he didn't complain. It was nice to be "mobbed" in such an unexpected way.

The usual crowd was there, however, just beyond the platform barrier. Irving said nothing. Ellin said only, "We had a lovely trip and we are perfectly happy. No, we have not made it up with my father." A waiting chauffeur took them directly to the Carlton Hotel in the Haymarket, a stone's throw from Piccadilly Circus. The *London Evening News* commented: "If all the Haymarket caught fire tonight, it would not draw Irving Berlin and his bride from the seclusion of the royal suite of the Carlton Hotel."

A gold-braided guard was posted outside the suite to screen everything but the food they ordered. He sized up would-be visitors, decided who was to be turned away, who deserved to have a message sent in, and who was privileged enough to be let in. Reporters tried dressing up as maids or waiters; others gave their names as Alexander Korda or C. B. Cochran. They were all shown their way back to the hotel elevators. Before long, the Cockney guard was issuing press statements of his own. "H'all I can say, gentlemen," he'd tell reporters, "h'is that they are supremely 'appy—if you get my meanin'."

After several days, the Berlins emerged one evening, blinked at the flashbulbs awaiting them, threaded their way to an elevator, and escaped to a car which took them to the brightest night spot of the era. At the Kit Kat Club, Sophie Tucker was saying farewell at the end of a record-breaking engagement. One of Berlin's generation, she first captured the public in the twenties.

The Berlins sat at a table by themselves until Sophie herself spotted them and asked that he come over to the piano. "If you play 'Remember' I'll sing it," she announced, and the night-clubbers clapped thunderously. Embarrassed, Berlin made his way to the spotlight and thumped a few notes as Sophie sang. Sophie then told the audience that she and Irving had known each other since he'd been a singing waiter and she just a young hopeful waiting for a break. He had played his earliest compositions just for her, she said. It was hardly true, but the audience loved it.

"It was the greatest smoking concert I've ever known," said one writer of the evening. Another noted, "With the arrival of Irving Berlin, the American conquest of the English stage is practically complete."

Berlin was soon planning an even broader conquest—a new show, to be put on at that most famous of all British theaters, The Theatre Royal, Drury Lane. He was going to work with Frederick Lonsdale. It would be a super, star-studded revue. By the end of January, the *London Daily Express* reported that bookings for the new Berlin-Lonsdale show were running into May of the next year.

Meanwhile, callers continued coming to the Carlton Hotel. Among them was an entire team of men delivering flowers. These particular bouquets, a gift from friends in the south of France, had taken up so much space on the express taking them across the Continent that it was dubbed "the Flower Train."

Only occasionally would Berlin unbend about personal publicity. A London music columnist cornered him and impressed him so much that Berlin said, "It's good to talk to someone who doesn't imagine me to be the hero of some wild romance, slipping out of New York over to England in rubber shoes. All I've done is get married and come over here on my honeymoon. I'm having a fine, happy time."

The interviewer was delighted with Berlin's brisk and invigorating way of speaking.

"I know nothing about music," Berlin told his listener further. "That is, I know nothing about the science of music. People think this is miraculous. They don't understand how a man who knows nothing about music succeeds in writing as much of it as I have."

Then he came up with an interesting analogy. "Look, your medium of expressing yourself is a typewriter or your pen. You come and talk with me and your natural ability to handle vocabulary enables you to go back to your office and write a conversation with me which allows thousands of people to see what sort of man I am, what I've got to say.

"But supposing you didn't have a typewriter or a pen—like Homer, for instance—you could still convey by your voice, at least, what you thought my ideas were. So without the mechanics of your profession you could, in a way, be just as good a journalist. I don't know how to put music on paper, but that doesn't prevent me from making music, from expressing myself in melody."

The next day the Berlins packed up for Paris. At his request, two pianos were moved into their hotel suite, one for the salon, the other for the bedroom. But no inspiration or thought, as he used to say, hit him either for his London show or for Tin Pan Alley. So he and Ellin decided to emerge from the hotel suite and face the music of photographers and reporters.

They strode out into the hall—but not a flashbulb popped. Instead, one man with a camera shouted at them, "Step aside, please!" Flabbergasted, they did. A horde of newspapermen brushed past them to corner a visiting maharajah at the other end of the hall. Reporters were so resigned to the idea of never seeing the Berlins that they didn't even recognize them in close-up.

With or without notice, Berlin was happy. He learned that the French Society of Composers had just paid him 44,000 francs on royalties for songs which had been played in cafes, cabarets, and restaurants. The French checks proved that "Remember," "Always," and "All Alone," all new Berlin standards, were being requested more than any home-grown product.

Meanwhile, a play of Ellin's had been accepted, helped probably by her newly achieved fame. But she didn't feel ready to go to work adapting it for production. For one thing, she was tied up with reporting assignments for *Vogue*, specifically on the latest rage, the Charleston. Flappers everywhere were high-kicking to the rackety new rhythm while their boyfriends' flannels flapped to the same tunes. In the U.S., one college had banned the dance because "plaster is being jazzed off the dormitory ceilings and pictures have tumbled down." Radios were ordered silent in the dorms because they were blamed for "that tired feeling in the morning." Ellin let *Vogue* readers know that she thought the dance, having captured high society, had also taught its members a very real respect for the chorus girl.

She explained, "To study the Charleston is to discover how much hard work professional dancing involves. . . . westbound streets [in New York] are clogged with smart motors bearing ladies to the Broadway dance emporiums. Some go anonymously in taxis. There are ladies who plan to say nothing of their studies until they can startle the world with their proficiency."

In New York rumors circulated that Berlin had an agent gradually pawning all of Ellin's jewelry while he and she were out of the country. That was the real reason he'd married her, went the stories, which were part of a carefully worked out swindle. A gang had managed to make replicas of Ellin's well-known jewels, and more than a dozen victims were persuaded to buy them as the real thing. The swindlers convinced their customers that Berlin had pawned the gems and did not plan to reclaim them.

In March 1926, the honeymooners spent a few days on the

Portuguese island of Madeira and were so impressed with it that they determined to buy a villa there. The island had inspired Berlin to write a new song, a foxtrot which he called "Always in April." "I think Portuguese music itself is beautiful," he announced.

He had another new song he was eager to have performed. An optimistic sort of song which reflected the kind of life Ellin and he could have once the hubbub of publicity died down. The song was made to measure, it was decided, for Belle Baker, who had the title role in the new Rodgers and Hart show *Betsy*. The Berlin tune which was slipped in among the Rodgers and Hart numbers was "Blue Skies."

At the end of March, the couple came quietly back from Paris to London without a single reporter bothering them. "Life here is really getting to be perfect," Berlin declared. By now they had something more personal than ever to keep from the public. Ellin was pregnant.

Whether or not it had anything to do with the contemplation of fatherhood, Berlin felt uninspired. "Jazz is dying," he lamented in a letter to Sam Harris. "People are swinging away from it."

He did write a tune, dedicated to Ellin, called "At Peace with the World," which Al Jolson recorded, and another song called "How Many Times?" Then suddenly an older Berlin song was in the news. A car salesman named Abraham Brown, who said he wrote songs as a hobby, charged Berlin with stealing a song he alleged *he* had written and called "All Alone."

Since Irving Berlin's "All Alone" had caused a sensation, the case was of avid interest to the public. Brown, filing for an injunction in Federal Court, declared that he had written "All Alone" in 1924, although he had never copyrighted it. What he had done, he told the court, was to take his lyrics to Jean Paurell, a scout for Berlin, who had promised to discuss it with his songwriter-publisher boss.

Thereafter, Brown claimed he had never managed to get to Paurell. Brown's lawyer said that his client had been inspired to write the piece after he and his wife had separated. The court threw out the claim. "No composer of Irving Berlin's stature," said the judge, "would stoop to stealing a few bars of another man's songs."

Other tangles arose over "Gentlemen Prefer Blondes." Berlin had written a song with that title following the success of Anita Loos's book. A nice song to be sung in a nice play by a nice young woman. The trouble was that two nice young women wanted to use it—for rival shows. Each said that Berlin had given her exclusive rights to the number.

One was the London musical comedy star Joyce Barbour, who was opening in a new show at the Vaudeville Theatre. The other was Broadway's Nora Bayes. Miss Barbour said that Berlin had given the song to her as a birthday present. Nora Bayes, on the other hand, said she had acquired exclusive rights to the number from Berlin's publishers in Britain, and she too intended to use it in a London West End show.

The matter was settled the day after the story broke in the British papers. "My dear Joyce," Irving wrote in a letter to Miss Barbour, "I returned yesterday from Torquay and saw in the papers that there was a little controversy going on over the performing rights for my song 'Gentlemen Prefer Blondes.' I am giving Nora Bayes another song. She is perfectly agreeable that you sing 'Gentlemen Prefer Blondes' as I promised you."

So Joyce Barbour was free to use the number in her show *RSVP*. But there was also the matter of the song title. Berlin's was not the only one on the market. "Regarding any other version of the song," Berlin continued, in an effort to pacify Miss Barbour further, "I think you ought to know that Miss Anita Loos, who wrote the book bearing this title, gave me the right to use this title for song purposes some months ago. I hope you will have no further trouble about this and that the song will prove to be worthy of the fuss."

The title itself has become part of the American idiom but the song never really did survive the fuss.

For Berlin there was still the Drury Lane epic to look forward to. Or was there? At the end of August, he and his librettist, Frederick Lonsdale, met again for discussions. Berlin walked out in disgust. In fact, with that he walked out of England too. There was no libretto, so there was no Irving Berlin show for the Drury Lane. He and Ellin took the train to Glasgow and sailed secretly for Quebec. The heir to the Berlin fortune had to be born on the appropriate side of the Atlantic, of course.

They booked passage as Mr. and Mrs. J. Johnston on the small Canadian Pacific steamer *Montnairn*. The Berlins had all of the passenger cabins on board. Six of them. Two of the rooms were used just for Berlin's music and for the one-key piano which he had brought over with him. It was an almost idyllic trip, until a member of the crew got wind of the passengers' true identity and radioed word to three New York newspapers. Berlin had sent a written statement to the press in advance: "We beg for privacy."

Now they drove to the Canadian coastal village of Alexandria Bay, where Berlin had vacationed in previous years. Captain Bob Fitzsimmons, who ran a boat-chartering business, was ready and waiting with the special boat Berlin had once equipped with a phonograph. "Just sail on," Berlin told him. "We don't mind where."

So the boat made its slow, steady way through and around some of the Thousand Islands. "How far, sir?" asked Fitzsimmons. "You know, I have to charge you fifteen dollars an hour because this is a really expensive boat."

"That's all right," Berlin said. "I think the song I've just finished will bring in more than five thousand. This is money well spent."

Max Winslow had recently bought a cottage in nearby St. Lawrence Park, and was lending it to the returning honeymooners eight months after he had seen them married in New York.

Reporters of course caught up with them. Berlin now looked relaxed in white flannels and a white silk shirt. "I hope everybody is as happy as we are," he told the newsmen pleasantly. "We only want a chance to be left alone." While Irving played golf, Ellin stayed secluded in the cottage.

In late August—Rudolph Valentino was dying of pneumonia and Gene Tunney and Jack Dempsey were getting ready for their big fight—the Berlins finally boarded a private drawing room on the train for New York. Papers there were again rife with rumors. The most persistent was that a wedding was planned for the couple at St. Patrick's Cathedral in an attempt to "legitimize" their baby in the eyes of the Catholic Church and soften the reaction of Clarence Mackay.

Berlin announced that the only appearances he'd be making were going to be with the road company of the new Marx Brothers show *Coconuts*.

Was there to be no new wedding because the couple wasn't happy? It was noted that Ellin was not staying at the West Forty-sixth Street apartment. "Mrs. Berlin is with friends" was all the papers learned.

St. Patrick's staff made its own inquiries. Cardinal Hayes looked into the matter and found that there had been no Papal dispensation for the marriage in the first place, whereupon the Cathedral Rector announced, "I know nothing about any ceremony here."

Then Berlin himself disappeared. His publishing office knew nothing about where he was. Rumors and counterrumors mounted. One had it that they were separating. The other was that the Vatican was about to authorize a marriage.

Berlin finally issued yet another written statement: "The reports that Mrs. Berlin and I are to go through another ceremony are untrue." There had been "unnecessary publicity" and he was impatient at the situation.

It was not until October 26 that Ellin again appeared in person, checking into a Massachusetts hospital. In hotels nearby, rooms were reserved for her husband and her mother, Mrs. Joseph Blake.

11

Easter Parade

CLARENCE MACKAY WAS ON a duck-hunting expedition when he heard the news. His daughter Ellin had given birth to an eight-pound girl. He made no official comment, but called off the duck-hunting and went fishing instead.

His former wife, on the other hand, had been present at the birth of Mary Ellin Berlin. "She is very pretty. The image of her mother," Mrs. Blake said proudly.

Berlin got back to work. With a newcomer on his family scene, he wrote what must rank as one of the most beautiful of all his tunes, "The Russian Lullaby."

The song was hummed, whistled, and sung not just in nurseries, but in vaudeville theaters, in nightclubs, and on the streets of a thousand towns all over the U.S. There was also criticism. How could a man who had escaped from Russia write a song like that at a time when public sentiment was anti-Bolshevik?

Berlin told his critics: "I look forward to a time when Russia will be free. My song is a lullaby, nothing more."

Years later, he was asked what decision had been the most important of his life. His immediate answer: "It was made for me by my parents. Their decision to come to America."

With his private life receding into the privacy of a newly acquired New York home on Sutton Place, Berlin was more able to concentrate on his career. "Blue Skies" became the big hit of 1927 and gave Berlin a place in history. Al Jolson sang it in the world's first feature-length talkie, *The Jazz Singer.*

In 1927, there was another Berlin hit but, ominously perhaps, it was called "The Song Is Ended." Suddenly, it appeared that the song really had ended for Berlin. A terrible depression broke over him. He went on writing songs. But if the melody of the old ones lingered on, there was something strained about the new ones. Once people had heard them, no one seemed to mind that the songs had ended. He wrote something called "In Those Good Old Bowery Days." He looked for inspiration in topicality and came up with "Why Should He Fly at So Much a Week When He Could Be the Sheik of Paree?" The reference was to Charles Lindbergh's transatlantic flight, but Berlin shouldn't have bothered.

Then he wrote a new score for the Ziegfeld Follies, his first in six years. "Shaking the Blues Away" was the show's hit and the best thing Berlin had done in months. Eddie Cantor and Ruth Etting were the stars. Yet *The New York Times* said: "Perhaps it was Mr. Berlin's score more than any other thing which informed the energies of these entertainers."

The new edition of the *Social Register* came out with no reference to Ellin or her marriage. "Irving Berlin," the *Register* commented coldly when asked about the omission, "has no position in Society."

The *New York Times,* however, thought them important enough to be included in their social news column, and made mention of it when the couple and two-month-old Mary Ellin left for Palm Beach, where they had taken a house.

Later the *Times* reported: "Radio science and the best-known composer of popular music collaborated last night in the production and dissemination of a ballad with a speed which was startling even in these breath-taking days.

"Until last night, the world had not heard Irving Berlin's latest song 'What Does It Matter?' and indeed until Thursday, Mr. Berlin himself had not thought of it. The composer, with his family, is in Palm Beach. Thursday night he composed his latest offering and at four o'clock he telephoned it by long distance to Nathaniel Shilkret, Director of the Victor Talking Machine Company's Salon Orchestra.

"Mr. Shilkret orchestrated the piece yesterday, and last night the voice of Lucrezia Bori, singing at Station WEAF, bore it out on the air through twenty-six other stations to perhaps ten million listeners in the United States and Canada.

"Mme. Bori's surprise number came in the midst of a suitable program in which she was joined by Giovanni Martinelli, tenor, also of the Metropolitan Opera Company, and Pablo Casals, cello."

Irving Berlin had made much more than gossip column news at a time when he was beginning to lose confidence in himself as a songwriter.

The unwelcome glare of personal publicity reappeared in 1928, when reports suddenly spread that Ellin was desperately ill. Ellin went horseback riding daily, but even the people who saw her couldn't quell the rumors. "It's ridiculous—here, talk to her yourself," Berlin said to one telephone caller. But even his wife's voice failed to satisfy people. Pernicious anemia was supposed to be the cause of her serious indisposition.

Actually, the only peril she was in was that born of the kind of celebrity she had become. When there was no more runaway romance, no suggestion of a religious marriage ceremony, and it was very plain that Clarence Mackay was still not reconciled, what else was left to fabricate?

That same year, one Ira Arnstein alleged that he had submitted a song called "Alone" to Berlin's publishing house, and that the songwriter had stolen it. He wasn't suggesting that Berlin had used the melody for "All Alone." He said he had used it, instead, for "Russian Lullaby."

"The music is plainly that of my song, which has never been published or copyrighted," Arnstein told the court in asking for an injunction to ban further sales or performances of "Lullaby." The case was thrown out of court.

In August of 1928, there were rumors of Berlin's setting up a home in Hollywood. This was the first inkling of a story that still hasn't completely died down. Every now and again, the story recurs that Irving Berlin's life is to be filmed. The picture is always going to be called *Say It with Music.*

When Joseph Schenck announced that Berlin would supply music and lyrics for a movie of that name for his United Artists Company—which had been set up by Chaplin, Mary Pickford and Douglas Fairbanks all of whom were out of the organization—the rumors seemed justified. When Schenck announced further that it would be the story of a songwriter, everyone of course thought it was going to be Irving Berlin's own story.

Berlin was quick to scotch such reports. "I am not going to have any film about me while I'm alive," he said then, and has repeated the remark at intervals ever since.

Rumors of a reconciliation with Clarence Mackay didn't die down either. They were given emphasis when the Berlins established their own estate at Sands Point, Long Island—not far from Mackay's palace, Harbor Hill—and heightened dramatically when Mackay's mother died. "He can't turn his back on Ellin now," people said. Indeed, at her grandmother's funeral, Ellin sat next to the father she had not seen for more than two years. Her brother John and sister Kay also shared the pew.

The papers had a grand time speculating. The *London Evening Standard* reported: "The last wish of Clarence Mackay's mother was that father and daughter should be reconciled," said the paper. "And when they came together for the first time, the financier took her in his arms and kissed her." In fact, the meeting was entirely strained. Clarence Mackay was not forgiving anything.

In September 1928, Berlin made his radio debut. The show, over WEAF, had a national reach of forty-three stations. It was the first of a series to be called—what else?—*Say It with Music.*

The programs were to help Al Smith's second campaign to get to the White House. Berlin was there with other members of the

Actors and Artists League for Smith. He had a new song for him, "Good Times with Hoover—Better Times with Al." He didn't just speak a polite sentence or two on the air, he sang all the lines of his "We'll All Go Voting for Al" and "Roses of Yesterday." There was also the pleasure of joining George M. Cohan on the same radio bill. His admiration for Cohan was as strong as ever, though he had long since eclipsed his former idol.

Smith was defeated. Berlin, though, had a personal triumph to celebrate. Ellin had had another baby, this time a son.

The Berlins were thrilled, but only for a few days. In less than a month the baby was dead. He died on Christmas morning of a defective heart.

Ellin's high-society friends now showed their true colors. Those who had seemed to welcome Izzy Baline so warmly, far from sympathizing with the bereaved parents, whispered that their son's death on Christmas morning was a sign of divine retribution. "It's God's punishment for marrying a Jew," said one devout Catholic.

For weeks Ellin was ill. Berlin took her to Florida to recuperate. He himself tried to forget by going back to work with Ray Goetz, his former brother-in-law. They were to present shows at The Music Box. The first was to be *Fifty Million Frenchmen*, with a book by Herbert Fields, music and lyrics by that promising youngster, Cole Porter.

Berlin had originally planned to do the show himself, but he had little feeling for it now. When it opened a year later, he inserted an ad in the papers calling it "The Best Musical Comedy I Have Seen in Years." The show, according to Berlin, "has more laughs than I have heard in a long time, and one of the best collections of song numbers I have ever listened to. It's worth the price of admission to hear Cole Porter's lyrics." That was praise indeed.

Clarence Mackay—who had at least sent a letter of sympathy to Ellin on the death of the baby boy—sold his controlling interest in the Postal Telegraph Company. The firm went to the giant ITT conglomerate and Mackay took his entire fee in company shares. It was the most foolhardy thing he ever did.

With the stock market crash in 1929, Clarence Mackay lost every cent he had. He still had his house and the magnificent grounds but couldn't afford the servants to help run them. One Wall Street writer counted his loss "the greatest reversal of fortune of any rich American." The year before, he had spent over a million dollars just on personal expenses, buying art treasures, paying little in taxes. Now there were paintings and his gold and silver to sell, but what price could he expect when everyone else was selling, and no one had the money to buy? Mackay closed down his Harbor Hill estate and moved into the porter's lodge, where onlookers described him as looking like "a retired English colonel who had seen better days."

Most of Berlin's money also went down the Wall Street drain. The past year had not been vintage Berlin by anyone's reckoning. His trip to Hollywood had produced some film theme music, and his "Puttin' On the Ritz" gave Harry Richman a signature tune that was to stay with him for as long as he was on the boards with a top hat to wear and a cane to twirl. But, "I was scared," Berlin wrote about the crash. "I had had all the money I wanted for the rest of my life. Then all of a sudden I didn't. I had taken it easy and gone soft and wasn't too certain I could get going again."

Later he said, "Perhaps the real dream job is being a failure. Then you don't have to worry about maintaining a standard."

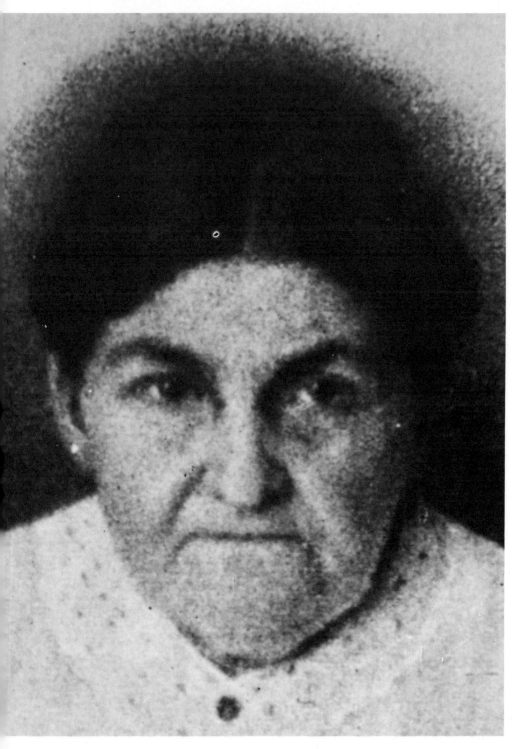

Mama Baline (*Radio Times Hulton Picture Library*)

Number 330 Cherry Street—where it all began (*Radio Times Hulton Picture Library*)

His first sheet music—the mistake that turned Izzy Baline into Irving Berlin (*Radio Times Hulton Picture Library*)

This is the life

Photo by

Berlin 1912. In a Friars Parade, proving he had very much arrived. (*Radio
Times Hulton Picture Library*)

(top) Irving with his mentor, George M. Cohan in front of the sign advertising a *Friar's Frolic* (*Radio Times Hulton Picture Library*)

(bottom) Irving, the dog lover (*Radio Times Hulton Picture Library*)

On board *The Leviathan*. Irving and Ellin face the cameras. (*Radio Times Hulton Picture Library*)

With Jascha Heifetz, both with hands on the black notes (*Radio Times Hulton Picture Library*)

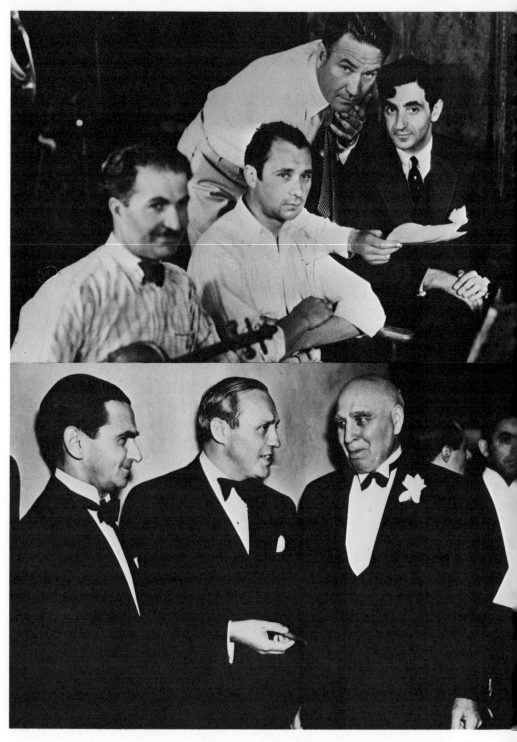

(top) Irving learning how his music is played for a film soundtrack in the '30s (*Radio Times Hulton Picture Library*)

(bottom) With Jack Benny—and Eddie Cantor hovering in the background (*Radio Times Hulton Picture Library*)

Two greats—and between them the masters of showbiz, Irving Berlin
and Al Jolson (*Leslie Kaye*)

(top) This is the Army. Irving backstage with General Jacob L. Devers and Lady Mountbatten. In the background—his 'boys'. (*Associated Press*)

(bottom) Irving fêted by Hollywood (*National Film Archive*)

(top) With Count John McCormack (*Associated Press*)

(bottom) On the air with the BBC in 1944—broadcasting in the Forces
programme 'Atlantic Spotlight' (*BBC*)

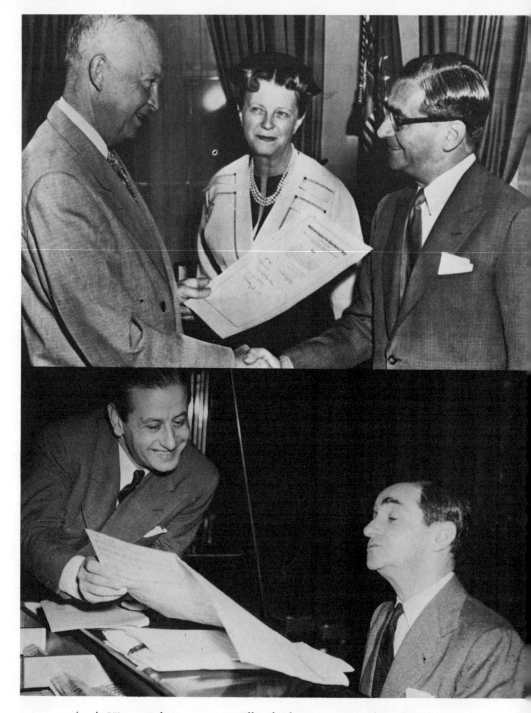

(top) His proudest moment. Ellin looks on as President Eisenhower presents Irving with the signed bill authorising a gold medal for the writer of 'God Bless America' in 1954. (*Associated Press*)

(bottom) In London showing how it's done—to bandleader Geraldo, who was playing a Berlin selection on the BBC Light Programme's 'Milestones of Melody' (*BBC*)

On the Riviera. With daughter Mary in 1955. (*Associated Press*)

Posing with daughter Elizabeth on the steps of St George's Church, Hanover Square, after her marriage to publisher, Edmund Boyd Fisher (*Associated Press*)

Doin' what comes naturally—playing the black notes at a rehearsal in 1966 for his updated version of *Annie Get Your Gun*—with fellow song-writer (and, in this case, producer) Richard Rodgers and his star Ethel Merman (*Associated Press*)

Irving Berlin at 80. A portrait commemorating his birthday in 1968.
(*Associated Press*)

12

Let's Face the Music

To those who believed that he played piano with only one finger, Berlin stressed that he used all ten—but badly. More than ever now, however, he was praised as "the writer who has written more hits than anyone else." "Yeah—and more flops, too," he'd quip.

And it did seem, as the twenties gave way to the thirties, that Irving Berlin was writing flops better than ever. If he hadn't needed the money now—he still had ambitions for bigger and better Broadway shows but had no cash to create them—it might not have mattered quite so much. If he hadn't had the constant fear that he'd never again hear people whistling and singing his songs, it probably wouldn't have mattered at all. But it did matter, and for all those reasons.

His last interesting work had been completed just before the Depression, a score for Al Jolson's picture *Mammy*. It was a maudlin, sentimental tale set around a minstrel show and is not remembered as Jolson's best movie effort. But one song, "Let Me Sing and I'm Happy," served for the rest of Jolson's life as his *cri de coeur* and as his epitaph when he died in 1950.

Styling a song for a particular entertainer's talents was a gift that was peculiarly Berlin's. Jolson was always Berlin's favorite entertainer and it was still something to have him introduce his tunes. The score for *Mammy* wasn't Berlin's best work. But one

119

song in it—"To My Mammy"—had more interest after it was sung than when it was first written and presented to Jolson. It contained the line, "How deep is the ocean . . . how high is the sky?" The tune flopped and that line in the middle of the lyrics was forgotten for years.

The film did, however, make Berlin some money which went toward building a $200,000 house on East Ninety-third Street. And royalties began coming in from old songs.

The Depression brought a flood of tunes for the breadlines. "Buddy Can You Spare a Dime?" not by Berlin, was successful enough to become a classic. Berlin wrote tunes for the age, too, but his were neither good nor successful. One, called "Just Begging for Love" was featured in the show *Shoot the Works,* which was produced to help starving performers. Noted one critic, "Berlin received nothing for this number and it was worth it."

The year 1931 was one Berlin might otherwise have liked to forget had it not been for a lawsuit involving Clarence Mackay. Someone named John Hansen sued the Postal Telegraph Company and the Commercial Cable Company in the Supreme Court. He said he had negotiated with the Mexican Government on behalf of the two firms and Mackay himself to put the companies' lines through Mexico. The deal went through, but Hansen didn't get his promised fee of $100,000.

What made the hearing notable was not only that Ellin Berlin sat next to Clarence Mackay in court but that she took the witness stand and demolished Hansen's case. She remembered Hansen well from a trip she and Mackay had made crossing the English Channel on their European "escape and forget" tour in 1924. She also remembered that no business of the alleged nature could have been discussed.

When the hearing was over, Clarence embraced his daughter for the first time since the elopement, and the meeting that newspapermen had been eagerly awaiting for five years took place in relative privacy. As Clarence Mackay and Irving Berlin shook hands, press photographers who had been hounding them for years were safely away on other stories.

Mackay was about to be remarried to Anna Case, daughter of a village blacksmith who had become a Metropolitan Opera prima donna. By the time the Berlins attended the Mackay wedding, it seemed the most natural thing in the world for them to do.

Berlin now wrote songs and put them away. "I don't think any kind of creator, of songs or stories, can work well if he knows that his stuff is just headed for the trunk in the attic," he once said, looking back at those times. "You have to feel that people are going to see or hear or buy what you've done. Maybe I'm a little too self-critical." Actually, he was much more afraid of having his work rejected by the public.

So Max Winslow went behind Berlin's back and paid a call on Rudy Vallee. Vallee was America's top radio star. His show *The Fleischmann Hour* got the top rating every Thursday. "Irving feels he's all washed up," Winslow told him. "But here's something of his I'd like you to look at and please, sing it for him." The song was "Say It Isn't So." Berlin had written it months before and then put it away in a desk drawer.

Vallee recorded it for his next broadcast. It was a show he particularly remembers. He heard the recorded program played back in his lawyer's office the night he and his wife Faye were planning their divorce. As she heard the song, tears rolled down Faye's face. "The lyrics said all I felt," said the singer himself.

"Later, Irving told me I had helped him to sort out his career. But he helped me save my marriage." "Say It Isn't So" has been recorded again and again for nearly forty years.

The success of "Say It Isn't So" gave Berlin the courage to bring out another song from under wraps. When "To My Mammy" flopped as a solo number in its own right, Berlin took the questions from the middle verse and used them as the opening lines and title for something called "How Deep Is the Ocean?"

"I always took lines and other bits out of bad songs," he told me. "And I'll tell you something else. All songwriters do. The only different thing about me is that I acknowledge it. Others don't."

"How Deep Is the Ocean?" gave Berlin back his self-confidence. Enough at least to contemplate a return to Broadway with a score for a new Moss Hart show called *Face the Music*. Two songs in the show stood out, "Soft Lights and Sweet Music" and the one that summed up his newly relaxed mood, "Let's Have Another Cup of Coffee."

For Moss Hart's next production, one of the tableaux needed a number to go with one of the year's great holidays. Berlin thought back as far as 1917 and that year's big flop "Smile and Show Your Dimple." In 1933, that flop became a super hit called "Easter Parade." The show it fitted so well was *As Thousands Cheer*.

Now that his self-confidence had been restored, Berlin still needed money. Not since the opening of The Music Box had he had to borrow. This time he was ten thousand dollars in debt.

He needn't have worried. His score and Moss Hart's book kept Broadway talking and the box office steadily busy. Berlin's forty percent profits (twenty percent as composer and twenty percent as lyricist) made him rich again. Rich enough, eventually, to bail his father-in-law out of trouble. He made him an unpublicized gift. Some of the people who moved in Mackay's much depleted circle at the time, put the figure on the check Berlin signed as high as a million dollars. Others doubled it.

Without knowing any details, a columnist wrote soon afterward in 1934, "Eight years ago, Izzy married the daughter of Clarence Mackay. There was trouble. Today there is peace. Izzy is richer than his father-in-law."

Interesting that the writer should have called him Izzy. It was a name that certainly helped convey the feeling of the situation, but Ellin had always made it very clear that only members of her husband's family, or people who had known him in his Bowery days could call him that.

It was "Easter Parade" which made the big impact on

audiences in *As Thousands Cheer*. But critics were quick to sound a sour note about the song. Even the *New York Times* agreed it was reminiscent of something else. "At the end of the first act," it noted, "there's a song (you may have heard it on the radio) called 'Easter Parade.' The surly muttered about its alleged similarity to the wistful little piece of years ago [1909] 'Put On Your Old Gray Bonnet.' The rumors reached Irving Berlin, who stood them for a time, as all songwriters learn to do, but the matter eventually ceased to be funny."

.The writer might have said that Berlin, of all people, would not have been amused in the first place. "The confusion results," the piece went on, "from the fact that 'Your Old Gray Bonnet' is rhymed with 'on it' and in 'Easter Parade' bonnet goes with 'upon it.' That's all."

But the man from the *Times* did recognize the similarity to "Smile and Show Your Dimple." Berlin told him, "I remembered my brain child, sat down one night and wrote a new set of lyrics, changed the end of the tune a little and let it go at that."

A huge backdrop for *As Thousands Cheer* featured the daily pages of a newspaper, and each number had a certain suitability for the appropriate day. One was "Heat Wave," sung by Ethel Waters. Marilyn Miller and Clifton Webb, who was a specialty dancer long before his "Mr. Belvedere" days, also starred. Another toe-tapping melody was, "I Wanna Go Back to Michigan."

"The reason I used Michigan," he confessed some time afterward, "was because it was the only way I could rhyme a place name with 'wish again.'"

Though he wouldn't always admit it, the entertainer in Berlin was never far from the surface. When radio became the great force that it did in the thirties, he was begged for his personal services. Singers had for years been performing his tunes over radio, but he himself was scared stiff of playing his piano or trying to raise his whisper of a voice in front of a microphone. He did finally succumb to an offer from the WJZ network, but insisted there be no studio audience. "A comedian may require a visible audience," he explained, "but it doesn't seem necessary for me. All I can do is speak with my songs."

He prepared to cover at least a hundred songs in his first five broadcasts, all to come under the inevitable theme of *Say It with Music.* He had carefully been studying radio for some time, secretly popping into studios and watching friends and other leading performers shaping up to the microphone. He knew that what most of them had was personality and an individual style. But after days of trying to perfect a style of his own, he gave it up.

"I'm appalled at the amount of preparation needed for each broadcast," he confessed, and got down to work, as ever, working best under the pressure of a deadline.

One thing in particular about the medium excited him. "Radio's most valuable asset is in the old songs," he declared, obviously pleased with the effect it was having on his bank balance. "The old songs are like old friends to the listener. Catalogues of yesterday's tunes are the backbone of radio today. On the other hand, a new lyric is more important today than ever before. Radio has made it so. The lyric enables the listener to remember the song if the title and tune are tied together."

A special department in the Berlin office kept track of the number of times his tunes were aired. Between 1932 and 1934, "Alexander's Ragtime Band" had been played by five stations 220 times. "Always" had gone out 104 times, "A Pretty Girl Is Like a Melody" had been broadcast 99 times. The beat-'em-all record was "Say It Isn't So" with 564 broadcasts and, not far behind, "Let's Have Another Cup of Coffee" with a score of 508.

The statistics impressed him favorably, though he told a *New York Times* writer that he couldn't understand why several of his million-selling tunes had not been broadcast a single time. Nor was he completely optimistic about the future. "Right now, after writing these broadcasts, I wonder how in the world radio can keep on going. Where will it get the material?"

Berlin was, of course, still turning out tunes, those produced by his one-key piano as well as those by other songwriters retained by his publishing house.

"It must be hell being Irving Berlin," said a rival publisher. "The poor guy's his own toughest competition."

Ever since his "Blue Skies" had been heard in the movies, Berlin had often been pressed to pack his bags and move to Hollywood. Equally often, he resisted. The film music he had done—the occasional theme tune, even the complete scores for Jolson and the Marx Brothers—had not really given him either enough personal satisfaction or monetary reward. MGM, however, made him an offer he thought made financial sense. He insisted on guarantees *and* on a share of the profits, which only Jolson had ever dared do before then. Songwriter Dave Dreyer reported: "Irving maneuvered all those sharpies in Hollywood as though they were Boy Scouts."

Arthur Freed, the MGM producer, said of Berlin's demands, "It took longer to write one of his contracts than a whole script. But after it was done, he'd forget about the contract and give you anything you wanted."

RKO was planning an all-talking, all-singing, all-dancing musical. Fred Astaire and Ginger Rogers were on hand for it. They had first met when starring in rival productions under the same management. All they needed was good material, and Irving Berlin was to provide it for them. First, he needed time to think —and, he suddenly decided, a new atmosphere.

With Moss Hart, he sailed for Naples on the Italian liner *Rex*. The old upright piano with the gear lever went along, as did the musical secretary.

They were in Naples for only eleven hours. But it was enough. Hart and Berlin spent most of those hours stretching their legs and watching the crew move their luggage and the piano off the *Rex* and onto the liner *Vulcania*.

By the time the *Vulcania* arrived in New York, Berlin was ready to pick up his family and move to Hollywood, where he was now sure he could best use his talents.

If he'd never before been accounted an absolute genius, *Top Hat* made him one almost overnight. There was not only the title number for Fred Astaire, "Top Hat, White Tie and Tails," but a marvelous tune called "Cheek to Cheek," a third, "Isn't This a Lovely Day to Be Caught in the Rain?" and a fourth, "The Piccolino."

Top Hat was a success wherever it played. People talked and wrote as much about Irving Berlin as they did about Fred Astaire and Ginger Rogers. Nowhere was the film and its music more appreciated than in Britain. Of "Cheek to Cheek" the *London Daily Telegraph* said, "Its success is the more remarkable because Mr. Berlin was the first and the greatest of the jazz composers." Berlin couldn't have put it better himself.

The percentage deal which produced that song was worth $285,000 to him. The success was all the more remarkable, in fact, because no one at first expected anything but dismal failure. That certainly was the reaction after the sneak preview of *Top Hat* at a theatre in Santa Barbara. The audience was restless. Halfway through the movie, one couple left, followed shortly by a dozen or more others. MGM was distraught, and Berlin looked all set for another bout of depression. But someone thought of arranging another screening. This time the picture had a sensational reception. "We played it before the wrong audience," said Berlin again and again after the experience which taught him never to trust previews. It didn't teach him, however, not to worry.

Top Hat helped cement a fast friendship between Berlin and Fred Astaire. "You can't work with Fred without knowing you're working for him," said Berlin. "He's a real inspiration for a writer. I'd never have written *Top Hat* without him. He makes you feel secure."

Berlin still wrote most of his music at night, though there were, of course, exceptions to this quixotic rule. Sometimes, sitting at a table in Lindy's with a friend, it took nothing more than the sound of an auto horn in traffic outside or a waiter's dropping of cutlery to bring an idea to mind. One evening he actually raced out of the restaurant leaving both a friend and his overcoat behind.

Another time, he spent the evening with Fred Astaire while the dancer waited in a Hollywood hospital for his wife to have a baby. To keep Astaire's mind off his troubles, Berlin spent the time playing gin rummy with him. "Say, what do you think of this for a tune?" Berlin said as if they had been talking song ideas all evening. "Yeah, I like it," said Astaire, after hearing Berlin hum it through. "Good," said Berlin. "Gin!"

"He had a good hand and a good idea for a song, and he used them both," said Astaire, looking back on the occasion more charitably than he may have felt at the time.

A year after *Top Hat*, Astaire and Rogers were together again in *Follow the Fleet*. Berlin had written the songs—"I'm Putting All My Eggs in One Basket," "Let's Face the Music and Dance," "Let Yourself Go," and "We Saw the Sea"—in close cooperation with Astaire.

Now, before an idea finally crystallized, Berlin would approach Astaire, whose artistry he deeply respected, with a suggestion. Astaire would visualize it, then pace it out in steps on the floor.

"I'd change just that little bit," Astaire would say. "You know—'dum-de-de-dum' instead of 'de-de-dum-de-dum.' "

"I think you're right." And Berlin would go off to try out the variation. With other songwriters, artists of Astaire's calibre could demand material. With Irving Berlin, they asked.

On January 31, 1936, 150 of America's foremost songwriters got together to pay tribute to this very different man among them. They gave him a testimonial dinner in honor of his twenty-five years of "leadership in our ranks."

The room in the plush hotel they'd chosen was transformed into a replica of "Nigger" Mike's old saloon in the Bowery.

Al Piantadosi, whose "My Muriuccia Take a Steamboat" had helped set Berlin on his musical course all those years before, was there to play the piano.

He played and Berlin sang, "Oh, How I Hate to Get Up in the

Morning," "Alexander's Ragtime Band," "Always," and "Cheek to Cheek."

Irving was asked to make a speech. Instead he did what he always did on occasions like this—he played a bit and sang more.

Hollywood was paying tribute to the man they hoped they could really adopt as their own. Al Jolson, Ernst Lubitsch, Joseph Schenck, Samuel Goldwyn, Irving Thalberg, and Darryl Zanuck were there among the songwriters to do him honor.

When the Berlins went to Britain for a holiday in 1936, they were greeted as royalty without the circus atmosphere that had surrounded them on their honeymoon ten years earlier. If he had been the King of Ragtime then, he was recognized now as Emperor of Tin Pan Alley.

But he was already mourning the early demise of melody. "Music is being carried prematurely to its grave," he said with not a trace of twinkle in the black eyes behind horn-rimmed spectacles. Radio, he had decided now, was the culprit. The *Daily Express* said he himself looked "as unmelodious as a lamp post."

Yet radio was helping to make him richer by the hour. Back in the U.S., he could look out of the window of his plush Manhattan home and say to a dinner companion, "Long way from Ellis Island, isn't it?" No one could argue the point.

The *New York Times* was still interested in the secret of his amazing productivity. "Everyone has a tune in his head," he told them. The reporter asked for a rough estimate of the number of songs he had written in a career of twenty-seven years as a tunesmith. "I believe I've written no more than 750 tunes."

To which the *Times* retorted: "You should be arrested for vagrancy!"

He wrote fast songs and slow ones, dance tunes and love ballads. As the head of a publishing house he had to watch his list. If there was a love song missing from it, he simply sat down and wrote one.

The rivalry among songwriters in those days was so marked that there were tunesmiths who would have given up songwriting before saying anything nice about the competition. Berlin more than once faced the acrimony of rivals, but he himself never behaved as anything but a guide and a friend.

He sent Cole Porter a letter to his home in France to congratulate him on "Night and Day." Wrote Berlin, "I am mad about 'Night and Day' and think it is your high spot. You probably know it is being played all over and all the orchestra leaders think it is the best tune of the year. I agree with them. Really, Cole, it is great and I could not resist the temptation of writing you about it."

Five years later, Porter came out with "Rosalie." A previous version of the number had been rejected by Louis B. Mayer and the new one wasn't, to Porter's mind, nearly so good. But Mayer liked the second version and it became a hit. "I wrote that song in hate," Porter told Berlin, "and I still hate it." Berlin replied, "Listen, kid. Take my advice. Never hate a song that has sold half a million copies."

The cynical might say that Berlin could afford to be generous. Everywhere he went, he was praised as the master, the king. But when Gershwin called him "the greatest American song composer," Berlin protested. "That was," he said, "going too far. He was a songwriter. Composer was altogether too grand a word."

This recognition of his own limits notwithstanding, Berlin would wince every time he heard music from the radio that bore little resemblance to what it had been when it left the Berlin publishing offices. An angry letter would go off to the offending bandleader or vocalist and legal writs were frequent.

Berlin was the first person, as far as anyone knows, to use the word "corny." "I suppose it means 'corn-fed' to us in Tin Pan Alley," he explained in the late thirties. "Nothing is so corny as last year's sophistication"—a sentiment Cole Porter might not have shared. But Berlin explained, "I mean corny lyrics. There's no such thing as a corny tune."

Nor was there such a thing as a totally unsalable song. Berlin never lost entire faith in his discards. In 1927 he had written a number which he filed away because "I thought it was so bad I wouldn't have it published." But ten years later, he decided the tune had something. It was called "You're Laughing at Me."

"I peddled it to Mr. Zanuck for a great deal of money . . ." and the tune became a tremendous hit. Dick Powell sang it in *On the Avenue,* Berlin's big hit picture of 1937 for Darryl F. Zanuck's Twentieth Century-Fox. The film included "I've Got My Love to Keep Me Warm," also sung by Powell, and "This Year's Kisses," sung by Alice Faye.

Life in the Berlin household had changed over the past few years. There were now three daughters. Besides Mary Ellin, there was Linda Louise, born in 1932, and Elizabeth Irving, born in 1936. Berlin's generosity to Clarence Mackay had, partly through his new wife's influence, brought about more than a thaw in family relationships. Mackay had a grudging respect for his son-in-law's ability to make money and to earn plaudits from the social circle Mackay respected so much. After all, Irving and Ellin had leased the shore house of a former U.S. Ambassador to France, and that couldn't be all bad.

In 1938, the Berlins went to Phoenix, Arizona, ostensibly for a seven-week rest. But the piano went with them. Within only a few days, Berlin had produced the entire score for a new Astaire-Rogers picture, *Carefree,* including the songs "Change Partners" and "The Night Is Filled with Music."

That autumn, Berlin went again to Britain. This time he was predicting the demise of swing. "It'll be dead in two years," he told the *Daily Express*'s Paul Holt, who described the songwriter as "rather like a wistful sparrowhawk. There is the questing beak, the beady little black eyes and the way of craning his neck back." Holt went on, "It is, in fact, amazing that with such a combination of characteristics added to a spare frame that does not top five feet five, the general impression should be one of dignity.

"Perhaps it is because you can't make him angry. You can say bitter, provocative things, talk about swing and the way radio has killed the music business in ten years—all this you know he hates, and yet he will answer mildly, if a little sadly, but with a complete understanding."

It was the year that Robert Donat walked off with all the movie honors for *Good-bye, Mr. Chips.*

Holt described Irving Berlin as the "Chip of Jazz." He was just over fifty. There certainly seemed something of the old man about him in the way he talked about swing. "I don't hate it that much," he said. "But it will die. Swing isn't music, it's just a way of playing it. Now they swing the classics and think they have something new. It's a fad. It'll die."

Radio and records? Ah, there Mr. Holt had struck a nerve. "They've made song hits into background music. Songs that were hits before radio are still hits. Songs that were made into hits by radio and films are forgotten. They still remember 'Alexander's Ragtime Band.' But they've forgotten my 'Cheek to Cheek.'" (That last remark didn't say much for the way Irving Berlin was keeping tabs on that aspect of the music business.)

In another interview he said, "We have become a world of listeners rather than singers. Music has been driven from our hearts to our ears. In the old days, Al Jolson sang the same song for years until it meant something. Records were played until they cracked. Today, Paul Whiteman plays a song once or twice or a Hollywood hero sings them in a film, the radio runs them ragged for a couple of weeks. Then they're dead."

London's hit at the time was "Doing the Lambeth Walk," and the songwriter Noel Gay told Berlin about another song he had written called "I Took My Harp to a Party." Berlin was instantly enthusiastic.

"That's the most poignant title I've heard in years," he told Gay.

"Poignant?" Gay asked, looking at Irving incredulously. "You can't be serious."

"Sure I'm serious," said Berlin, not a little offended. "Certainly I'm serious. 'I Took My Heart to a Party'—that's wonderful."

Gay said he thought songs had as much of a chance of suc-
ceeding in 1938 as they had at any time before. "But radio won't
let them," Berlin countered. "If I wrote 'Remember,' 'Always,' or
'What'll I Do?' today, they wouldn't be hits. Radio wouldn't let
them be."

He kept to his theme. "Ragtime is on the beat," he told
newsmen. "Jazz is off the beat. And swing has no beat at all. I don't
think it is music at all. Radio has brought about over-production
and over-distribution."

From London he told *The New York Times:* " 'Remember' took
three months of persistent plugging before we realized we had a
hit. But as soon as it caught on, it went up like a fever chart and
stayed at the top for a year. If I had written 'Remember' today, it
would have been played and forgotten in a month or so, if it
clicked at all."

He didn't like radio. But there was no recorded comment from
him on another headline in the same day's edition of that paper:
"Uncle Sam Eyes Television, Mindful of Its Possibilities in War-
fare."

13

Now It Can Be Told

By the late thirties, Berlin was being recognized as the elder statesman among songwriters—and he was enjoying every minute of it.

The biggest tribute to him had come from Twentieth Century Fox, which had produced a film that everyone thought was Berlin's own life story. It wasn't, but it was the first of a series of movies featuring nothing but his music—old songs and a mixture of new ones. In fact, in some ways it was little more than an excuse to play the melodies.

The film was *Alexander's Ragtime Band,* starring Alice Faye and Tyrone Power, the couple who at that time seemed to be in every other film Hollywood produced. Ethel Merman was in it, too, as were Don Ameche, Jack Haley, and a crowd of lesser-known singers. They sang not only the title song, but also twenty-seven others, including "All Alone," "Blue Skies," "Easter Parade," "Everybody's Doin' It," "When the Midnight Choo-Choo Leaves for Alabam'," and even "We're on Our Way" and "I Can Always Find a Little Sunshine at the YMCA" in a sequence reminiscent of *Yip Yip Yaphank.*

The story, based loosely on the adventures in and out of love of a bandleader named Alexander and his female vocalist, was nothing spectacular. What made the film special was Berlin's

133

music. It was as though Berlin himself had invented a new kind of entertainment.

No one talked about it as "Alice Faye's picture" or "the new Tyrone Power film." It was Irving Berlin's—every inch of the way. That was as it should have been, for the movie was, in a sense, a celebration.

Berlin had been writing songs for thirty years, a fact no one who had a radio could possibly have ignored. Every time one tuned in, someone was playing or singing a Berlin tune. Those who knew of Berlin's comments on 1938 broadcasting could have been forgiven if they had accused him of biting the hand that was feeding him very generously indeed.

On August 3, 1938, just as the picture was opening all over the United States, Irving Berlin himself was brought to the microphone. He didn't like radio now any more than he ever had. But with America's top stars gathered to pay tribute to him in New York, Chicago, and Hollywood, he couldn't turn down the invitation.

A Morse signal prefaced the greeting: "Good evening, Mr. and Mrs. North America and all the ships at sea. Let's go to press. This is your New York correspondent, Walter Winchell. . . ."

The news flash the familiar voice announced was that the biggest stars in American show business were gathering to celebrate "a dark, slim, wiry little fellow whose songs we have been singing for thirty years." The occasion would begin with "a word of admiration and affection from Mr. and Mrs. Winchell's little boy Walter." Inevitably, "Say It with Music" followed.

Al Jolson, the emcee, called him "the man who has written more hit songs than anyone else, the fellow who really leads the parade."

When Berlin came on, he did what he had always done on occasions like this. He didn't make a speech; he sang it, or at least he tried. The engineers had to adjust the knobs on their sound equipment to catch his voice—a voice of which the stuttering comedian Joe Frisco once said, "You've got to h-h-hug him to h-h-hear him."

Berlin stepped to the mike. "What can a songwriter say? What can a songwriter do? A fiddler can speak with his fiddle. A singer can speak with his voice. An actor can speak with his tongue in his cheek. But what can a songwriter say?"

The answer—the applause of the audience and the songs—lasted more than an hour.

Jolson introduced another show-biz giant—who had had his biggest break singing one of Berlin's tunes on the stage of Hammerstein's Victoria Theatre in 1909: Eddie Cantor. "Everything I've done and everything I've got out of life came from 'My Wife's Gone to the Country,' " said Cantor.

Berlin began to forget his embarrassment and unwind.

"Why don't we see what Berlin can do with his own songs?" suggested Jolson. "What key do you want?"

"You mean you have to have a key?" asked Berlin.

"All right, what note do you want it in?" Cantor quipped.

"That black one over there," came the reply.

And with that, the three of them sang "Mandy" in harmony.

Sophie Tucker recalled the days when Irving, as a singing waiter in Chinatown, gave her songs he had written on his cuffs. Bandleader Ben Bernie came on to pay tribute to the "Little Napoleon of Song." Rudy Vallee sang "Say It Isn't So." Tommy Dorsey came on from Hollywood to play "Marie," swing-style—and Berlin appeared not to wince at all.

Louella Parsons and Darryl Zanuck carried on a dialogue about the film, and the whole program ended with Ethel Merman, Alice Faye, and Tyrone Power singing tunes and doing sketches from *Alexander's Ragtime Band*.

Edmond O'Brien commented on the performance, "A great many songs have been born and died. A good deal of swing has swung through the years since Irving Berlin wrote 'Alexander's Ragtime Band' back in 1911, but the man who wrote that memorable tune has never allowed time and changing tastes to usurp his place in the front row of Tin Pan America."

When Berlin went to England for the film's opening, the BBC wanted to do a similar show, but it didn't come off quite as easily. The songwriter arrived amid rumors of copyright trouble between Twentieth Century-Fox and Berlin's London publishers, Chappells.

The problems were resolved, but until ten days before the broadcast, it wasn't certain that Berlin would give the go-ahead. Finally, the lawyers stopped arguing and the show went on.

Although the *Daily Express* had no high praise for the film itself, it knew where the nuggets lay: "Every cinematic cliché as it comes up is covered by the ingredients of the producers, who insist on covering it up with one of Mr. Berlin's more memorable numbers. It is nice not to have to worry how bored you are with boy-meets-girl, boy-loses-girl. Every time the yawn comes, so does Mr. Berlin to remind you by his melodies of some great point in show business."

Back in the United States again, Berlin realized he was getting more and more impatient with Hollywood. He acknowledged it had been good to him, but, he said, "I feel slow in Hollywood. The tempo there is slow. So I think it is good once in a while to get back to the theater. I have the feeling that if I don't get back, I'll never see Broadway again." It was his farewell to the film capital.

But before he went, he was asked to contribute to a commemorative anthology. A year earlier, Irving and Ellin had entertained George Gershwin and Kay Swift at dinner. During the meal, the young composer complained of a blinding headache—so painful that he had to be helped out. Two days later, Gershwin was in the hospital, and soon after that, he was dead.

Gershwin had once described Berlin as "the greatest American songwriter." Now everyone wondered what Gershwin himself might have done had he lived beyond his thirty-eighth year.

In many ways Berlin had been a model for Gershwin. "He has

vitality, both rhythmic and melodic, which never seems to lose its freshness," the younger man had said. "He has that rich, colorful, melodic flow—the envy of all who compose songs. His ideas are endless. His songs are exquisite cameos. Each one is as beautiful as its neighbors."

When Berlin was asked to contribute to the anthology, it was almost by way of reply. It was, he said, "a songwriter's tribute to a man who wrote wonderful songs."

Berlin and his wife were going back to New York. Irving had a new show to write—but there was another, more personal family reason. At the age of sixty-four, Clarence Mackay had died, on November 14, 1938. Because the two men had recently worked out most of their mutual animosity, Berlin was able to show support for Ellin when she really needed it.

14

God Bless America

CHAMBERLAIN HAD COME BACK from Munich with a promise of "peace in our time," and the immediate danger of war over Czechoslovakia seemed to have passed. But Europe's war clouds had affected America's mood, too, as Berlin discovered when he got home.

Kate Smith, the big, jovial singer who had become famous with "When the Moon Comes Over the Mountain," asked Berlin for a patriotic song to sing on her weekly radio show.

Sensing the times, Berlin had for days been trying to come up with just such a tune, and for days he had been throwing them in the waste basket. Then he dipped into his mental index which, in turn, led to his filing cabinet. He brought out a sheet, yellowed and frayed, that had been stored with the material for *Yip Yip Yaphank*. It was a number he had rejected because he thought it would be overdoing the show's finale, a song called "God Bless America." He made some minor changes in it and took it to Kate Smith.

"I tried to write something new," he told her, "but I found I was too close to all that is happening in Europe. How about this?"

"How *about* it?" Kate exclaimed after a few minutes' study. "You've just written a new 'Star-Spangled Banner'!"

Neither of them guessed how right she was. Within days of her first broadcast of that song, it had not only shot to the top of the Hit Parade, but people had begun to sing it in groups. When the band played it at the start of a ball game at Brooklyn's Ebbets Field on Memorial Day, the crowd stood up and the men took off their hats. Berlin had indeed written a new national anthem.

Kate Smith recorded the song and sang it at the New York World's Fair in 1939. Its title became the most popular catch-phrase in America. People wore buttons or waved pennants bearing the legend, "God Bless America."

In 1940, both the Republicans and the Democrats announced that they were going to use the tune as campaign songs at their presidential conventions. Berlin was clearly more in favor of the Republicans' adopting it, although he gave his blessing to President Roosevelt's workers, too. Learning of GOP plans for the song, Roosevelt's committee chairman declared, "Why should we alter *our* plans? Wendell Willkie probably will use 'The Star-Spangled Banner,' too."

Berlin refused, however, to allow dance bands to play the piece. "Their intentions simply aren't patriotic," he explained. Eventually he ordered that "Only Miss Kate Smith and the GOP have permission to sing 'God Bless America' whenever they please."

He wanted none of the royalty money. His purpose had been to glorify the country he loved. The money would go to a charity, and he duly set up a trust fund to administer it. The man he put in charge of the trust was Herbert Bayard Swope, the New York reporter who, more than thirty years before, had given Berlin the first of thousands of press notices. All Berlin stipulated was that the money be used for patriotic purposes among the youth of America. So Swope brought in Colonel Theodore Roosevelt, son of the former President, and boxer Gene Tunney. With Berlin's happy agreement, they decided that the charity to benefit from the song would be the Boy Scouts and Girl Scouts of America. It was to make the movement rich. And it created a bond between Berlin and the Scouts that has never loosened. From the time the trust fund was announced, the song was used to begin the day in many public and Sunday schools.

Today, Berlin says: " 'God Bless America' is the song that means more to me than any other. It was the first song I'd ever written which required no push to get it started. I can't say why. Perhaps it is its quality as a home song. Perhaps it was because of the state of world affairs then."

The *New York Times* commented on the phenomenon in July 1940. "Americans who found 'The Star-Spangled Banner' hard on their voices have found a patriotic song they can sing. Its words are simple. Its music has only an eight-tone range."

But it did not please everyone. From a New York City pulpit, the Rev. Franklin Ronig suggested that Americans were using God's name "too readily" when they sang.

"Mingled with much that is good in the spiritual composition of our people," he said in a sermon, "there is a strange and specious substitute for religion held by many in times of crisis like the present. This finds its expression in the mawkish iteration of snatches of a song like 'God Bless America.' The great national anthems that have lived and that will outlive most contemporary doggerel came out of the hearts of men who knew what it was to sacrifice for America."

Writing to the *Times* in July 1940, Herbert Bayard Swope rushed to Berlin's defense. "I am Chairman of the God Bless America Fund, the fund receiving all the royalties flowing from the song. These royalties, which amount to $50,000 already, have been donated to the Boy Scouts and Girl Scouts. Irving Berlin, composer of this song, has known tragedy and misfortune. As a child in arms he was a fugitive from persecution in Russia, finding in America a haven of refuge and hope. Millions of his fellow Americans now sing his song, I dare say, with greater avidity than the struggle through the 'Star-Spangled Banner.'

"That, of course, remains, and always will, our national anthem. But when the Rev. Dr. Ronig says the 'Star-Spangled Banner' came out of the hearts of men who knew what it was to sacrifice for America, I wonder if he was referring to the melody.

"That, as he should know, was a ribald drinking song called 'Anacreon in Heaven.' I wonder why the Rev. Dr. Ronig, with so much to engage his clerical attention, chose to pick on 'God Bless America' ?"

Taking a different tack, the *New York Times* editorialized, "First place among patriotic songs in 1917 easily belonged to George M. Cohan's 'Over There.' Today, Irving Berlin's 'God Bless America' seems to be emphatically in the lead. That these songs of a nation should emanate from the two most eminent masters of their times is not in line with common tradition. Patriotic chants that sweep a nation or war songs to the tune of which millions march to battle are usually the work of humble or unknown authors. Custom-made songs by Poet Laureates seldom find a hearing . . . but in the case of Messrs. Cohan and Berlín we have the exception."

As late as 1940, Berlin couldn't have been more pleased to have his name thus coupled.

Two years later, he was still drawing crowds with his "anthem." He led a school band in a rendition of it as youngsters presented New York's Mayor Fiorello La Guardia five million signatures pledging aid to "I Am an American Day."

"The reason 'God Bless America' caught on," he told S. J. Woolf in the *New York Times Magazine,* "is that it happens to have a universal appeal. Any song that has that, is bound to be a success. And let me tell you right here that while song plugging may help a good song it never put over a poor one." So spoke an expert. The mob, he was sure, was always right. "It seems to be able to sense instinctively what is good and I believe that there are darned few good songs which have not been whistled or sung by the crowd."

Soon after, Berlin and Alexander Korda, the Hungarian-born British film producer, were sharing a taxi down Fifth Avenue one day. At about Fifty-eighth Street, Korda asked Berlin if he had any new shows in mind or even a new song. At Fifty-seventh Street,

Berlin started to hum. By the time the taxi reached Fifty-second, he nudged Korda. "Say, listen to this—do you think it'll do?"

"This" was "It's a Lovely Day Tomorrow." Korda looked at him and smiled and Berlin sat back, relaxed. It would do all right. So did the new show on his mind.

Berlin had left Hollywood and come back to New York, but the idea of a comeback on Broadway was a nagging one. He hadn't done anything in the theater for seven years and it was hard to think of creating another box office smash. But Buddy De Sylva, a fellow songwriter turned producer, had talked out a rough story idea about an imaginary territory in which corruption is so rampant that the U.S. government begins an investigation. Morrie Ryskind wrote the book, Berlin the songs, and the show became *Louisiana Purchase.* "It's a Lovely Day Tomorrow" was the hit of the hit show and almost as popular was "Fools Fall in Love."

If Irving's political leanings in the 1940 presidential election were Republican, Ellin wasn't content with just casting her ballot for the Democrats. She was actually making campaign speeches for Roosevelt. (Clarence Mackay would have turned in his grave.)

At one open-air rally in midtown New York, she took along a stepladder to serve as her personal rostrum, transporting it to the meeting in the trunk of her car. "Roosevelt is the man we all want," she shouted from the top of the ladder, "the man America needs." Then she got down from the ladder for a moment to drive home additional points. As soon as she had vacated the ladder, though, a taxi driver mounted the steps and shouted in support of her arguments, "Roosevelt has cut unemployment by seven million!" That annoyed another cab driver, who heard it in passing, pulled over, and demanded that he have equal time on the makeshift rostrum. "You damned Reds," he shouted.

A crowd gathered, traffic snarled to a halt, and Ellin Berlin had to get back in her car and hope it would all blow over. The row died down only when the anti-Roosevelt cabbie got hailed by a fare. Ellin retrieved her ladder and went home.

She had given up magazine reportage and found herself a new

and passionate interest. She joined the Committee to Defend America by Aiding the Allies—very left-wing, some people thought. She couldn't have been more dedicated. In one memorable radio debate she defined her position clearly, and made the wife of another American celebrity the target of her feelings.

Anne Morrow Lindbergh had written a book called *The Wave of Terror,* in which she seemed to sympathize with Germany. On the air, Ellin described the wife of the famous aviator as a "sensitive and gentle woman who has been bewildered and frightened by skillful German propaganda."

The question being debated: "Is Propaganda Endangering the U.S.?" Mrs. Berlin had no doubt it was. "Some propaganda *is* dangerous," she said. "Propaganda that confuses us and weakens our will." And she said, "Propaganda was part of the German strategy of terror."

She drummed the point home hard: "Look at *The Wave of Terror* by Anne Lindbergh. No one can be blamed for being frightened, but it is heartbreaking to find an American woman burying democracy in quotation marks. She speaks of it tenderly, but she speaks of it as though it were dead, drowned in that wave of tyranny against which inevitability Mrs. Lindbergh refuses to fight. That is not true. Democracy is alive here. It is alive in England.

"The Nazis have disguised old-fashioned tyranny to look like something new. They have touched the heart of a poet like Mrs. Lindbergh.

"In this war," Ellin went on, "Mrs. Lindbergh would have us believe that there is a conflict not between good and evil but between the old and the new. A man has led his people out to conquer. There is nothing new about that. Democracy is a lot newer than tyranny. I do not believe that liberty and good will must be overwhelmed by men of evil will. And that is what it is, the wave of the future to which we are told to submit.

"It is the will of men who intend to conquer the earth by

bombs and planes and guns. We must not romanticize the Nazis; they are not a wave. They are a group of unscrupulous militants who mean to conquer the world. 'Today we rule Germany, tomorrow the world.' That is what they say. That is not what I say."

Irving had caught Ellin's fever. Previously his forays into politics had been limited to writing songs and hearing them played by bands at political conventions. Now he was deeply concerned by what was happening in Europe. He made huge donations to Jewish relief work. And he wrote a song about the little man with the Charlie Chaplin moustache called "When That Man Is Dead and Gone." The following month this advertisement appeared in *Variety:* "No One Can Stop These Hits—'When That Man Is Dead and Gone' and 'A Little Old Church in England.' "

The *Daily Express* in London thought that the second tune had been inspired "by how we can take it."

In November that year, Berlin composed a song for the American Red Cross which became the organization's official anthem. "Angels of Mercy" he called it. It was as corny as Berlin himself might have complained. But the Red Cross liked it. Said its Chairman, Norman H. Davis, "Mr. Berlin has written a song which vibrates with the deeper meaning of the Red Cross and we are proud to have it dedicated and presented to us."

Soon after Pearl Harbor, Secretary of the Treasury Henry Morgenthau, Jr., asked Berlin to follow up his previous song, "Any Bonds Today," with an appeal to collect a record income tax total in the first spring of the war, 1942. The copyright was assigned to the Treasury Department.

The fact that it wasn't the usual Irving Berlin blend didn't alter favorable public reaction to the song. Imagine getting the public steamed up about paying income tax. But Berlin did it.

15

White Christmas

ONE OF IRVING BERLIN's fancies had become, as a less than sympathetic observer put it, to "corner the market in American holidays." "Easter Parade" had long since become as traditional as colored eggs; no appropriate radio show was ushered in without it. "God Bless America" now seemed standard for the Fourth of July. For Christmas, though, what could challenge Christmas carols?

Then Paramount Pictures brought Berlin back to Hollywood to score a new Bing Crosby–Fred Astaire film they were calling *Holiday Inn*. He came up with the theme song early on. "Happy Holiday" seemed to say everything the movie needed. But the word "Christmas" began to nag at Berlin.

Just which songs were to be used in the film was left very much to Berlin. He would have discussions with the team, director Mark Sandrich, one of the musical directors, Walter Scharf, and arranger Joe Lilley. But the songs themselves were to be Berlin's.

Though he worked closely with the other musical people on the set, a stipulation was written into the *Holiday Inn* contract that not a note of his music would be changed once filming started. There would be no chance he might not recognize his own music once everything was locked in the can.

He did much of his composing in Walter Scharf's office. It was there he installed his one-key piano and plunked away while

Scharf kept up with the notation and later prepared it all for orchestration.

"We thought 'Be Careful, It's My Heart' was going to be the big hit," recalled Scharf later. "But a few days after he had given me that song, he came up with another one. It seemed nice enough but no one thought it would be much else."

That nice enough piece was "White Christmas." A scene in the picture called for a number where Bing Crosby, feeling depressed, was trying without success to sell a nightclub. Sitting pensively at a piano he launched into how much nicer it would be to celebrate a real Christmas with snow, not the festival he was used to spending under the palms in Beverly Hills. Crosby sang it on his radio program when the film was released late in 1942 and the rest is history. But if no one else knew the song was going to be a tremendous hit, Berlin himself did.

Composing it, he had sat in Scharf's little room oblivious to what was going on around him. Scharf rushed in occasionally to answer the telephone. Berlin wasn't even aware of its ringing.

When the piece was finally orchestrated, he was told not to bother to come in until Bing was ready to go before the cameras.

"Don't worry, I won't," he said. But at nine o'clock the next morning, he was there waiting for work to begin.

"Irving, don't bother to stick around," Scharf told him. "We won't be ready for quite a while. Don't waste your time."

"All right, all right," Berlin answered.

Finally, the first chords of the verse were struck and Bing Crosby was in place, ready to dub the song.

"It was just then that I noticed that one or two of the flats—you know, the screens we use to dampen the sound—were out of place," recalls Scharf. "I went behind to investigate and there was Berlin bent low, trying not to be seen."

"I'm sorry," he apologized. "I just had to stick around."

Berlin sat in on all the story conferences and discussed with Bing Crosby, who had first sung Berlin's music as a boy in

Spokane, Washington, just how he wanted every one of his songs interpreted. With Fred Astaire, he went into intricate detail on the choreography of each number.

When the early days of shooting got underway, he was on the Paramount lot every moment, watching with an eagle eye. But he was in New York when a problem came up over blending one scene into a sudden change of season from winter to spring. Joe Lilley wanted a modulation of notes, but he knew that Berlin's contract was so watertight that even for an operation as simple and standard as that, he would have to get Berlin's personal say-so.

He phoned him in New York. "I tell you what we're going to have to do, Irving," said Lilley. "We'll get to the end of the song and on one note we'll dissolve to the next scene."

Berlin answered, "Just so long as it's one of *my* notes."

It was during the making of *Holiday Inn* that it became apparent just how eager Berlin was to keep his reputation both on Broadway and in Hollywood. A studio executive came in to the lot one day with a copy of the *New York Times*. "That play we were talking about is doing fantastic business on Broadway," he said. Berlin acted as if the remark had been a personal affront. "What do you mean?" he said sharply.

"Why get mad?" asked the executive. "It's no competition to you. It isn't even a musical."

"Well, it's too bad it *isn't* one of my shows," Berlin answered and stalked off.

But there were days on the set when he was fantastically pleased, particularly when he heard "White Christmas" as it was finally orchestrated. "He lay down all sorts of laws," Bing Crosby told me. "But he was very enthusiastic and somehow everyone else caught that enthusiasm. He'd make you share it. He wrote what was right for his singers. I'm lucky to have had him."

One of the things Berlin disliked about Hollywood was that it took so long to get a public reaction to his tunes. On Broadway he'd know on opening night, but he had to wait a whole year till the audiences paid their money at box offices to see *Holiday Inn*. It was August 1942, before anyone heard Bing's rendition of "White Christmas."

"It came out at a time when we were at war and it became a peace song in wartime, nothing I'd ever intended," Berlin said years later. "It was nostalgic for a lot of boys who weren't home for Christmas. It just shows that inspiration can produce anything."

But certainly neither Irving Berlin nor any other songwriter could imagine just what sort of inspiration "cornering the holiday market" with "White Christmas" could be in terms of cash value.

More than seventy million copies of the song have been sold in records and sheet music, thirty million of them of Bing Crosby's recording alone. In the 1969 Christmas season, the last year for which records are available, it was estimated that Berlin earned $60,000 from it in the space of a few weeks.

It is widely recognized today as the second most popular Christmas song the world has ever known, second only to "Silent Night."

As Bing Crosby said, puffing on his pipe and relaxing on the set of *Holiday Inn*, "I don't think you need to worry about this one, Irving."

16

This Is the Army, Mr. Jones

With the shattering of the fleet at Pearl Harbor and the entry of the United States into the war, Irving Berlin offered to make his own unique contribution to the war effort: a sequel to *Yip Yip Yaphank*. The deal was fixed in Washington. The Army would release the men Berlin wanted for a new show and the money it took would go to Service charities.

Berlin made it clear that he didn't have any intention of taking a penny from the show himself. But to him the question of copyright was always a burning issue, and the United States Government couldn't grant itself a copyright. So a special company was set up, This Is the Army, Inc. The title of the show that Berlin decided on, *This Is the Army*, seemed to him an obvious one.

He was now fifty-three and no more keen to wear a uniform than he had been twenty-four years before. But he did want to get the atmosphere of this new Army. There was nowhere better to absorb it, he felt, than at Fort Yaphank. So the Army moved him into a bare room at Camp Upton and shipped his one-key piano to him, along, of course, with someone to do the notating. The piano had done so much traveling by now that Berlin called it his "Buick." Since he never touched the white notes, they had their own vital purpose of serving to hold the cigarettes he now chain-smoked. Some keys were so yellowy-brown that they bore little resemblance to the originals. He had other one-key pianos, but the Buick was his favorite.

Berlin and the Buick were welcomed warmly to Camp Upton. No one looked at his haircut or sized up the way he wore his gaiters. Instead, the general came out to greet him as he settled into his new "office." It was all very different from 1917. Or was it?

The men still wore helmets, although they were now allowed thinner shirts and had ties to go with them. And they still had names for sergeants whose parentage they doubted. None of them liked getting up early either.

Early in his new stay at Camp Upton, Berlin decided there was something different about the new crop of soldiers. He told newspapers that "they have seen many of the ideals of 1918 shattered. They are more serious and grim now." But he said they had one thing in common with their fathers, their patriotism, and that made Berlin feel good. Just as he had decided in *Yip Yip Yaphank* that it would have been gilding the lily to feature a number like "God Bless America," he was again going to steer clear of anything blatantly flag-waving. As in 1917, he concentrated his songwriting around the men and their attitudes.

The cast was again going to be drawn exclusively from servicemen. The War Department had agreed to that providing that whatever entertainers Berlin wanted for this military operation were not allowed to forget that they were still in the Army. This was made patently clear by the opening phrase of the title song, "This is the Army, Mr. Jones, no private rooms or telephones."

Sitting in that cramped room at Upton, Berlin decided on one exception to the cast's being exclusively Army. There would be one civilian in the production wearing an old 1918 Army tunic and singing "Oh, How I Hate to Get Up in the Morning" just as he had before.

In addition to his Buick, Berlin had an almost equally antique portable typewriter sent to Upton on which he could peck out the lyrics he was concocting for the show. As with everything else, it was to be the most important thing he had ever done. Commanding officers throughout the nation were ordered to gather the talent for Berlin's personal inspection. He wanted singers, dancers, comedians, jugglers, and, in many ways most important, female impersonators. Again this was going to be an all-male show, but again he needed men who with the aid of strategically placed oranges or padding would really look like women.

When he wasn't auditioning, he was writing, pacing the floor of the lonely room, smoking cigarettes and scorching the ivories, and humming melodies to the music stenographer.

There was an old chrome chair in the room on which he would sit as he pecked out numbers and from which he would jump whenever a command was shouted to the troops outside. An order from a sergeant could make him change the course of a lyric or fire him to start an entirely new melody. If the weather was unkind, the only warmth came from an old black enamel stove. Since it was just like the stoves in hundreds of barracks across the country, that, too, could keep his imagination lighted.

The room was locked. The only distractions he wanted were the sounds outside. It was one time when Berlin did his composing during the day, wearing a polo shirt and slacks. Horn-rimmed glasses and a cigarette drooping from his lips completed the dark figure of concentration.

The newspapers knew what he was working on. He recognized the value of publicity, if only to ensure that the best talent really would find its way to him. But when he did see reporters, he was as intense and as anxious as he had ever been.

"Sergeant Berlin Re-enlists," one magazine titled a story and "The Army Takes Berlin" headlined more than one newspaper.

When he wasn't actually writing, he'd take long walks through the compounds of the camp to the infirmary or simply drop into the canteen for a cup of coffee with the men. He watched a boy hungrily eating a sandwich and that gave him an idea. Another time, seeing a Negro on parade resulted in his production of an all-black number called "What the Well-Dressed Man in Harlem Will Wear."

For weeks on end he deserted Ellin, but by May 1942, he was ready with his score and a cast of three hundred. Most of the cast were unknowns though some, like Burl Ives, made names for themselves later on. Others included Staff Sergeant Ezra Stone, who had starred as pre-war radio's Henry Aldrich, Jules Oshins, who wrote only "Have tuxedo—will travel," on his audition questionnaire, and Gene Kelly's brother Fred, who also became a well-known dancer.

Berlin knew he had been right about going on location to get his production under way. "You can't write a song out of thin air," he told a magazine interviewer. "You have to know and feel what you are writing about. A good song embodies the feelings of the mob and a songwriter is not much more than a mirror which reflects those feelings." The men at Camp Upton, for instance, were singing "This Is the Army" to themselves before anyone else had heard it.

Sergeant Ezra Stone supervised rehearsals with Berlin not only in Upton's "Opry House" but in a succession of Broadway halls and theaters. Getting rehearsals organized is difficult enough in peacetime with a civilian cast. But with *This Is the Army*, the men not wanted on stage were ordered to the nearest parade ground or to an armory for weapons training. So it was quite possible to be dancing in the morning, firing rifles in the afternoon, and back on stage, dressed up as a woman, in the evening all with official Army sanction.

Though the financial affairs of Irving Berlin were going to take a prearranged knock (the entire box office take, and sheet music and record royalties were going to the Army charity), he was avidly interested in everything, particularly in how the orchestra was tuning up to present his music. He may have been helping the Army Emergency Relief Fund, but he was as meticulous as ever about preventing any liberties from being taken with his songs. He looked carefully, too, at the costumes and the magnificent scenery all designed by soldiers. He made sure early that everything would be all right.

He said, "If I can manage to put into words and music the feelings of the kid from Podunk and the one from the Bowery—and both have the same kinds of feelings, if I can catch the enthusiasm and the humor which often hides behind serious faces and the heartaches when their thoughts go back home, then I'll have something."

He had something all right, and he knew it even as he slept on the Army cot in the bare room adjoining his workshop. He knew it more certainly when, after rehearsals, the first real performance of the show took place privately in the "Opry House."

When it opened at the Broadway Theatre on July 4, 1942, it *had* to be the Fourth of July, there were no doubts about it at all. Ellin hugged and hugged him after the performance. He knew it had been wonderful from the cheers of the throng who had paid $45,000 to the newly set up Army Emergency Relief Fund to attend. The posters and the program for the performance billed the producer of the show as "Uncle Sam."

Under-Secretary of War William Patterson attended opening night, as did representatives of all the Services (including hundreds of soldiers who got in free) and of the City of New York. Just as at any other Broadway opening, a heavy sprinkling of people from show business came. Kate Smith had bought two tickets and, as if somehow repaying a debt to Berlin, paid ten thousand dollars for them.

Edward Fitch Hall, writing in the *New York Times Magazine*, said, "The little song writer has far surpassed the service hit of a generation ago." He particularly liked the "girl" dancer who, "though a bit hairy-legged and satchel-footed by ordinary Broadway standards, yielded nothing in grace to the dancer who wears skirts off-stage as well as on."

All the critics liked the rousing title song, as well as soft numbers like "I'm Getting Tired So I Can Sleep" and the lovelorn "I Left My Heart at the Stage Door Canteen."

The show had delightful moments of comedy, too, most of which could be appreciated even by the non-uniformed members of the audience. Nothing brought a bigger laugh than Private Julie Oshins' comment to his sergeant, "Go ahead, break me. Make me a civilian." It became one of the most quoted quips of World War II.

And no one brought louder cheers than Sergeant Irving Berlin himself, on stage in his World War I costume, having to get up in the morning.

Chief of Staff General George C. Marshall sent this letter:

Dear Mr. Berlin:

Last night you and the cast of your show faced perhaps as critical an audience as you will find on your tour. The ovation which you received I hope you find some measure of reward for the great talent and the tireless effort which all of you have devoted to *This Is the Army*.

In addition to expressing my appreciation to you for contributing to Army Emergency Relief and for providing an effective stimulus for civilian morale, I thank you for an electrifying evening in the theatre.

The *Saturday Evening Post* described Irving Berlin as "the happiest man on Broadway." And John Chapman wrote,

Of all the sparkling audiences of Broadway's first-night history, this one was the Five-Star Final Tops. For most of the evening, the select had been beating their hands together with unaccustomed violence. But all this was just a warm up. On stage, a big fellow named John Murphy suddenly snarled, "Berlin. Where's Berlin?" It was the sort of demonstration that made you want to cry, it was so good. If you had been that little guy, you would have busted right out in tears. You'd have been so overwhelmed, you'd have come apart.

His is the only voice I ever heard that is at once squealy and husky. But on that night he would have drawn audiences away had Caruso been singing across the street. The only thing that can stop *This Is the Army* is the end of the war.

Berlin said of the show, "It's the biggest emotional experience of my life. Nothing has ever matched this."

There were, of course, uncharitable side effects. Ticket brokers complained that *This Is the Army* had broken the established "theater code" by compelling them to buy a certain number of tickets for the first two weeks of the show's life, but on a sale or return basis. A. L. Berman, Berlin's lawyer and president of the agency looking after the show's business affairs, said that this had been done to avoid having scalpers buy up certain desirable locations. Berman finally cut the number of tickets allowed to brokers so that there'd be more seats available at the box office.

Not long afterward, songs from *This Is the Army* were temporarily banned from U.S. airwaves. Singer Lawrence Tibbett, President of the Federation of Radio Artists, complained that four planned broadcasts of the show were providing unfair competition to professional radio personalities, even though advertising profits were all going to the Army Emergency Relief. Tibbett declared, "None of our members has ever refused to do anything for the Army and we think there are much better ways of raising a few paltry thousand."

Paltry? A. L. Berman answered that the ban would prevent $40,000 from going to the fund rather than into the coffers of Chesterfield cigarettes, scheduled sponsor of the shows in question.

Sniping from others in Tin Pan Alley hurt Berlin most. It was implied by some that the whole thing was nothing but a massive publicity campaign for Irving Berlin. The money he was losing by giving it to charity was simply the amount he would have had to pay in fees for self-promotion. It hurt, of course, because Berlin genuinely intended the show to represent his own war effort.

Cole Porter sent off a typically warm letter,

I can't understand all this resentment of my old friend, "The Little Grey Mouse." It seems to me that he has every right to go to the limits towards publishing the music of his Army show as every cent earned will help us win the war. If I had my way he would have been given the Congressional Medal, because even you must admit he is the greatest song writer of all time—and I don't mean Stephen Foster.

It's really distressing in these days of so much trouble to know that envy still runs rampant even on Tin Pan Alley. I'm sure you will agree about this, dear little mouse.

Love, Rat Porter.

While some sniped, others played a different game: trying to spot the talent in the show's lineup. Men in the cast were soldiers, but to Broadway talent scouts, they were potential entertainers. Night after night, scouts were there with their notebooks and, if they managed to bypass security, were at the stagedoor after each performance with tempting offers of what could be after the war.

It was as much a treat to hear the orchestra as to watch the acts on stage. Berlin had gathered the best of instrumentalists from the bands of Paul Whiteman, Red Norvo, Tommy Dorsey, and Buddy Clark. Dance critics like John Martin called the choreography "never less than workmanlike and it sometimes goes beyond that to touch high points of imagination and skill." Private Robert Sidney and Corporal Nelson Bardift, who directed the dancing, "had the good judgment," according to Martin, "to let those dancers with specialities exhibit them without interference. As a result there is considerably more variety in the choreography department than most Broadway shows can boast."

A newly formed organization called the American Theater Wing War Services Inc. gave a luncheon at the Hotel Astor for Berlin and the cast of *This Is the Army*. Broadway's queen, Helen Hayes, presented a gold cigarette case to Berlin. It was, she said, "crammed with the esteem, love and admiration of the American Theater Wing War Services and the hearts of the cast and members of the profession."

This Is the Army was due to run for four weeks. After two extensions, it finally left the Broadway Theater, on September 26, after 112 performances.

That was really only its beginning.

The show went on to Washington and then to California, where filming began. Jack Warner, who had signed the movie contract before the show even opened on Broadway, promised that every penny of profit would, like the stage show's, go to the Army Emergency Relief. There would be only a twenty percent "distribution charge" and if there were a profit on distribution this, too, would go to the Army. "When I signed the contract more than a year ago," Warner said in June 1943, "Mr. Berlin said he expected the potential gross of the stage production would be $250,000. Instead, the gross for the show's first ten weeks in New York and nineteen weeks on the road was around two million." Before long, that two million dollars seemed like chicken feed, too.

But other things were coming from Berlin's old "Buick" while the money from *This Is the Army* was being totaled. There was "I Can't Tell a Lie," which Fred Astaire sang on Washington's Birthday, and "I've Got Plenty to Be Thankful For," from Bing Crosby on Thanksgiving Day. Berlin was continuing to "corner the holiday market."

He agreed to adapt his song "Any Bonds Today" to help the Australian Government raise a war loan with all proceeds benefiting the Australian Armed Forces.

To some, he seemed to have a copyright on all wartime music. At a nightclub one evening with Ellin, he heard someone shouting at him, "Play 'Praise the Lord and Pass the Ammunition.' "

"But I didn't write that," he shouted back.

Others in the audience took up an insistent request. "If I don't play," Berlin told Ellin, "people will say I'm jealous because I'd like to have written such a hit . . ." Ellin nodded agreement.

So he got up and walked over to the piano where he did his best to play the Frank Loesser tune.

When *This Is the Army* moved on to Hollywood, Berlin had only one concern about the screen adaptation. "Just don't change the songs," he ordered. The music and lyrics went unchanged. But two numbers were dropped and one added. Kate Smith was brought to the screen to sing "God Bless America." A deal had to be worked out, juggling with percentages and profit margins, so that the royalties from this would as always go to the Boy Scouts and Girl Scouts.

Top cameramen donated their services for this movie to Army Emergency Relief; Associate Producer Hal Wallis and Director Michael Curtiz refused to take salaries, and so, of course, did Producer Berlin.

For the movie, Berlin donned his old World War I uniform and sang "Oh, How I Hate to Get Up in the Morning." Just as the recording of the number was completed, one electrician leaned over to his partner and whispered, "If the guy who wrote this song could hear the way *this* guy is singing it, he'd turn over in his grave."

Nonetheless, the *New York Times* saluted Casey Robinson's screen story, which linked *Yip Yip Yaphank* with *This Is the Army* through a father-and-son experience, and thanked him for giving his services. "But the best intentions cannot always make a good show, and it is an all-important fact that *This Is the Army* is one of the greatest musicals ever done on stage and screen.

"These soldiers have the freshness, the vitality, and the look of the Army one sees everywhere. They seem as intimate and real as the kid around the corner. One feels a good deal of pride watching them—bright and decent and funny. They are the greatest thing in a great show. If this be praise, we hope Warners make the most of it."

In the movie version, real girls had been added where needed, and a few better-known male names gave glitter to the original cast. There was Sergeant Joe Louis, Lieutenant Ronald Reagan, and dancer, and future senator, George Murphy. There were also veterans Alan Hale and George Tobias, as well as Joan Leslie, Dolores Costello, and Frances Langford.

Ellin was doing her morale-boosting bit too, helping to set up USO units all over the U.S. and in overseas battle theaters, to "keep alive the hearts of our fighting men."

"USO Clubrooms," she declared, "provide a service that the Government could not supply, because we are not a regimental people and Government supervision of such activities would not fit in with our idea of freedom."

Meanwhile, *This Is the Army* was getting ready to go on tour. First stop, London. To Berlin, it seemed an obvious place, but there were many who doubted the wisdom of it. Huge numbers of American servicemen living among the British, in preparation for the invasion of Europe, had bred a string of resentments against the Yanks. Most of it stemmed from the fact that they earned more money, six or seven times as much as their British counterparts. Among other things, this meant they could afford to give the girls a better time than the Tommies could, and that caused the most resentment of all. The U.S. Army had become a public relations problem in Britain, though no one would have called it that in 1943.

So *This Is the Army* was opening at that shrine of British vaudeville, the London Palladium, not just to entertain, but to ameliorate. All money raised would be for British servicemen. Berlin brought only 169 men to London with him. Basically there were to be no real changes except for one song, which was to demonstrate the special relationship between the two countries.

As soon as he arrived in Britain, Berlin realized that the one he'd written was too syrupy for Anglo-American relations as they really were. A story was going the rounds about an American senior officer getting on a London bus and offering his fare to the woman bus conductor. She told him that the bus was full. "But I've got to keep an urgent military appointment," he said. "Don't you understand that the outcome of the war depends on us?"

"Pardon me," replied the conductor, "I didn't recognize your Russian accent."

But Berlin wanted a special British song, one that would make a perfect finale for the Palladium show.

He went for a walk in the blackout, sat in the pubs for awhile, then strolled through the streets of the West End and got hopelessly lost in Piccadilly. He went back to his hotel, had a hot bath "and by the time I was through with the bath, I had it all worked out." What he had worked out was a song called "My British Buddy," and the next day it was in rehearsal at the Palladium.

Opening night, Berlin himself croaked with the chorus about the British and the American servicemen, each of whom thought himself responsible for winning the war.

That good-humored verse raised more than ten thousand dollars (the fee the English publisher paid) for British Service charities, opening night. And it brought the house down.

On stage, Berlin got down on one knee for a reprise and clasped the microphone to his chest. "I've got to sing it this way or you'll never hear me," he told them. Then he added a bit of personal philosophy: "Life is ten percent what you make it, ninety percent how you take it." They loved that, too.

The newspapers also liked it, and one remarked that it was the cleanest show seen at the Palladium for years. To the *Daily Herald*, it was a show which "kicked London sideways." The *Daily Mail* called it a "riot." Two days after the opening, the *New York Times* reported that "My British Buddy" was having the desired effect. "A new song is sweeping over London and its psychological punch is equal to another big chunk of Lend Lease."

On opening night, Lord Louis Mountbatten's wife Edwina made a speech from the footlights expressing her gratitude for the help Berlin was giving to the British Service charities. She and Lord Louis had already established a personal rapport with Berlin. Both Mountbattens were great lovers of America, where they had spent their honeymoon, and there was something else, too. Lord Louis was the son of Prince Louis of Battenberg, the man whose large tip had been politely declined by young Izzy all those years before. When Berlin and the Mountbattens had lunch together later Berlin joked, "I see I'm not the only one here who's changed his name."

At that same lunch, as a matter of fact, Berlin mentioned an unanticipated problem he had had with "My British Buddy." He told the Mountbattens he had gone to Louis Dreyfus, who owned Chappells, his British publisher, and told him he wanted $10,000 for the song. All the money would go to charities, he said.

"You can have the money," Dreyfus had told him, "but perhaps you could first tell me where I'll get the paper to print it." Britain's paper shortage was so acute that newspapers were not allowed to print more than a single sheet folded into four pages each day.

"Don't worry," Lady Mountbatten said when she heard the story. "I'll get it for you." And she did.

Even the Royal Family came to see the show. The Queen told him afterward, "I've never seen anything like it. 'My British Buddy' brought tears to my eyes."

"Thank you, Ma'am," Berlin replied. "I wrote that song in the bathtub."

About a third of the seats at every performance were reserved for servicemen who didn't pay a penny to get in. But there was still a scramble for seats among people who were only too willing to help swell charity funds. "And now that the Royal Family has seen it," said a New York newspaper in a letter from London, "the scramble may become a dangerous stampede."

There's no certainty that Winston Churchill ever got involved in the stampede. But one day in late 1943, a letter came to Berlin's suite at Claridge's that bore the Prime Minister's crest and insignia. It was an invitation to join Mr. Churchill at Number 10 Downing Street.

Berlin was ushered into an ornate room, offered a cigar and given a glass of brandy. He had grown used to celebrities over the years but appreciated the importance of this visit. It was a warm welcome.

But once the preliminaries were over, Churchill grew intent

and serious. "What's your view of war production in the United States?"

Berlin stammered an answer. "Oh, we're doing fine." There was silence for a bit.

Then: "What do you think of Roosevelt's chances for re-election?"

Again, it wasn't the sort of query Berlin expected, but he was game, "Oh, I think he'll win again."

"Good," said the Prime Minister. "Good."

"But in fact, if he doesn't run again, I don't think I'll vote at all."

"You mean," said Churchill, "that you think you'd *have* a vote?"

"Well, I sincerely hope so," said Berlin, increasingly uncomfortable over the whole conversation.

Churchill appeared to be incredulous. "How wonderful it would be," he said, "if Anglo-American cooperation ever reached the point that we could vote in each other's elections. Professor, you must come for lunch some day."

Professor? Berlin was then shown the door, without mention of *This Is the Army.*

Professor Isaiah Berlin, economics expert at the British Embassy in Washington, was in London for a stay. That's who the Prime Minister thought he had invited.

When the show finished its London run, Berlin took the company on tour around the country. After eleven weeks, it had been seen and cheered by 25,000.

For one who saw it as a small boy, it remains a treasured memory.

17

My Defenses Are Down

BACK IN THE U.S., Berlin hardly bothered to unpack his bags. To an astonished gathering of the press, he revealed that he and the show were off again for Italy and Algiers.

This time, the audiences were to be made up exclusively of servicemen. When he arrived in Naples he was asked in a radio broadcast, "Is it true that the only man you've left behind is the fellow in the box office?"

"That's right," said Berlin. "There'll be no tickets sold for any performance. The seats and the house are free. You can't buy your way into this show over here. All you need is to be wearing the uniform of any one of the Allied Nations."

(In the final accounting, *This Is the Army* benefited the Allies by $9,800,000.)

"In 1918," Berlin reminisced on the radio, "the boys in the trenches sang together. But the fellow in the foxhole is not apt to sing by himself." So saying, the idea of a song for a foxhole intrigued him, and when *This Is the Army* opened at the Royal Opera House in Rome, Berlin finished the performance with his own high-pitched rendering (his voice had been compared to that of a "frightened foghorn") of a new song, "There Are No Wings on a Foxhole."

While in Rome, he followed General Alexander and a group of Allied soldiers and got an audience with Pope Pius XII. He was emotional and nervous during the interview, which was set up by an Army chaplain. But he said he had gone there for a reason: "I had heard many stories in Rome of the help the Pope had given the Jews and I took this opportunity of thanking the Pope." There was no way for him to know what later years revealed: that the Pontiff had missed opportunities to do exactly what Berlin was thanking him for.

The fifty-six-year-old songwriter admitted now that he was feeling "terribly tired." But he added, "I'm not as tired as a lot of guys." And that was why he had written "Wings on a Foxhole."

"I'd never have done that song if I hadn't been over there with those boys," he said. "You can't write a song out of thin air. You have to feel what you're writing about."

In addition to giving two "official" shows a day, Berlin gave impromptu performances at thirty-five base, field, and general hospitals. To an audience of Italians, he recalled how he, as a Jewish boy, had sung Italian songs. And then he led the crowd in a selection of old favorites.

"Of course the men gripe," he said about the GI's overseas. "Griping is part of Army life. But as long as a man has enough energy to gripe, he has enough interest to fight. Any Army that doesn't gripe is a losing one."

Even abroad he was still conscious, as the war entered its last year, that he was the self-appointed American songwriter laureate. People in the Philippines wrote asking him to write a song for them. He answered almost by return mail with a number called "Heaven Watch the Philippines." It was presented to their Government at an official ceremony in Manila. Later, he wrote a song for the school children of that country which he called "God Save the Philippines."

"Some kids had heard 'God Bless America,' " he said, "and thought it was a song I had written especially for them. I hated to tell them it wasn't, so I decided to write one that was." In the true spirit of the song's ancestry, proceeds from the song went to the Philippine Boy Scouts and Girl Scouts.

When sheet music to "My British Buddy" first appeared, it bore this note: "The performance of any parodied version of this composition is strictly prohibited." But before long there was "My Russian Buddy, He says he's winning the war and that's O.K. with me," and "My Irish Buddy, He's as neutral as can be." And in England there was "My Yankee Buddy, He gets ten bob a day, and I get two and three."

There were reports that Moscow Radio had translated the title song from *This Is the Army* into Russian and was using it as one of its signature tunes. Berlin registered no official complaint.

On the way back from Italy, Irving stopped off in Ireland to entertain at Allied bases near Belfast, and to go down to Dublin to meet singer John McCormack.

Three months after the end of the war, President Truman announced that Berlin was to be awarded the U.S. Medal of Merit. General George C. Marshall, then Army Chief of Staff, pinned the medal on Berlin's jacket. The ceremony took place in the Pentagon in the presence of a number of high-ranking officers. General Marshall told them the award came after a "three-year period from February, 1942, when Irving Berlin gave all his time to the creation of *This Is the Army.*"

The official citation read: "He has set a high standard of devotion to his country and has won for himself the thanks and appreciation of the U.S. Army for highly meritorious service."

The presentation followed the final performance of *This Is the Army* in Honolulu, October 22, 1945. It was as much the end of an era as of a show.

Berlin was by now so admired as an American "culture hero" that he had chances to meet people he would never have heard of in his Tin Pan Alley and Bowery days. On one occasion he was introduced to composer Arnold Schönberg.

"I'm glad to meet you, Mr. Schönberg," he said. "I've heard so much about your songs."

The eminent gentleman looked at Berlin and said something like, "Well, isn't that nice to know."

Years later, Berlin said apologetically, "Well, how should I know that Schönberg was one of those *real* composers? After all, I'm only a songwriter myself."

Back home at last, Berlin the family man could spend time with his loved ones. He felt bad that he had neglected them over the previous two-and-a-half years. "I wish we'd all kept scrapbooks," he said wistfully.

Ellin had just had a novel published. Called *Land I Have Chosen*, it was described as a "story of a modern Becky Sharp." *Time* magazine dubbed it "by any standard a remarkable first novel."

Irving couldn't resist calling up a local bookstore to find out how it was selling. He smiled broadly when he got the figures. "You're ahead of Somerset Maugham," he told Ellin.

Later he reminisced, "Can you imagine? If one of my songs had sold better than one of Kern's, I'd be walking on air."

The remembrance of *This Is the Army* will always be with Berlin, of course. "No one can describe the feeling you get from playing before audiences of as many as 17,000 young men and seeing and hearing their enthusiasm," he's said. "It's just overwhelming."

From New York he went back to Hollywood briefly, to score a new picture for Paramount with Bing Crosby and Fred Astaire. The film was *Blue Skies*, a kind of re-cap of earlier Berlin. There was the title song and "A Pretty Girl Is Like a Melody," "How Deep Is the Ocean?" "I'll See You in C-U-B-A." "Always," and, appropriately for these early post-war years, "I've Got My Captain Working for Me Now."

There was a new song too, "A Couple of Song and Dance Men" for Crosby and Astaire, which proved how well he could still write a song with particular artists in mind. There were also "A Serenade for an Old-Fashioned Girl" and a charming number he had scribbled in London, called "You Keep Coming Back Like a Song." It was a year, of course, before the movie was released. Again, the bane of Berlin's life for that year was having to wait so long between a tune's conception and its birth before a mass audience.

Then suddenly there was a much bigger and more exciting project offered to him.

18

Doin' What Comes Natur'lly

It was in 1945 that Irving Berlin got a call to go to one of New York's city hospitals. He arrived in time to be the first recipient of the news that his old friend and rival, Jerome Kern, was dead.

Not long after the funeral, Richard Rodgers called on Berlin. Rodgers and his partner, Oscar Hammerstein II, were producing a new show which Kern had been going to write. Now they wanted Berlin to take it over.

Two years earlier, Rodgers and Hammerstein had turned Broadway upside down with their *Oklahoma!* It had killed off Ruritania and every other stock idea that had once been known as musical comedy.

Now they had a book in the *Oklahoma!* mold, another Western story, though this time with greater emphasis on comedy. It was the story of Annie Oakley, the gun-toting girl who had shown pioneers that she could shoot as well as any man. Would Berlin write a score for *Annie Get Your Gun?*

"I can't write that sort of hillbilly music," Berlin told Rodgers. "Why don't you do it yourself, Dick?"

Rodgers' answer was plain, "We're too highly committed with a new show of our own."

Berlin and Rodgers talked further about the prospects for the deal on a Friday. That evening, Irving, Ellin, and the three girls took off for their fifty-six-acre farm in the Catskill Mountains. The following Monday he had lunch with both Rodgers and Hammerstein.

"We hope you've changed your mind," said Rodgers.

"Well," said Berlin. "I've read the book and written a couple of tunes."

The tunes were the romantic "They Say It's Wonderful" and a comedy number which proved that Berlin was as much a hillbilly as he had ever been an Italian, or a soldier, "You Can't Get a Man with a Gun."

Early conferences were held at Oscar Hammerstein's house. Listening intently, Berlin sat on the edge of a chair. When the idea came for a song, he would tap it out on a table in front of him. Again, he was chain-smoking with concentration. On another weekend, he disappeared into the Catskills and came back with five songs.

Annie was so much a part of him now that he cancelled a provisional arrangement to go to Hollywood to make a new film. By the time that the production "firm" was ready to talk about casting, Berlin had written "Anything You Can Do I Can Do Better," "The Girl That I Marry," "My Defenses Are Down," "Doin' What Comes Natur'lly," "I Got the Sun in the Morning," and "I Got Lost in His Arms."

One point in the show presented a special problem. Berlin was asked to fill in a "stage wait," when the scenery was being changed and something had to be done to keep the action going in front of the curtain.

He puffed more cigarettes, chewed gum, and banged at the Buick's black keys. What he came up with was "There's No Business Like Show Business." Over the years since, that number has been accepted by the theater in much the same anthem-like way that "God Bless America" became accepted by the United States at large. Although no one has been seen to stand up and take off his hat on hearing it played, it makes you feel like doing so.

Yet it might have ended up in the Berlin filing cabinet simply to gather dust. When Berlin presented his score for the second round of rehearsals, the number was conspicuous by its absence.

"Where's that 'Show Business' thing?" Hammerstein demanded, certain he had mislaid it among the pile of papers handed to him by the songwriter.

"I left it out," Berlin said sadly.

"In heaven's name, why?" Hammerstein asked.

"I didn't think you liked it," Irving answered. "You didn't say enough."

Later, Hammerstein recalled, "He was just going to throw it away. Now, out of context of the play, it's merely the song that *means* show business."

Never before had Berlin or anyone else written a score for a show that had as many hits as those he turned out for *Annie*. As Hammerstein remarked at one of the early story conferences, "Irving has no sophistication about it. He just loves hits."

Someone else who saw the way things were running when *Annie* was about to go on the boards said, "This isn't an integrated score. It's more like a succession of hit numbers." Irving was worried and annoyed about that. "What's this 'integrated'? " he asked. "Take almost any song from any show and you can cue it into any libretto."

Not that even with this blockbuster of a production there weren't disappointments. One of the sweetest, most "Western" songs in the whole score was rejected simply because there was no room to fit it in. The song, "Let's Go West Again" was dropped first from the original stage show and again from the film version even though Judy Garland went as far as recording it for the soundtrack. Now only a delightful recording by Al Jolson remains to show what a gem it is.

When it came to casting, Berlin held out for Ethel Merman for the title part in *Annie Get Your Gun*. "I want her because when she sings you can hear the words of my lyrics in the balcony," he told Rodgers and Hammerstein, and they agreed. A whisper from La Merman could sound like a shout from anyone else. Annie became her part the moment she opened her mouth and hoisted up her rifle as she first walked on stage. It was an inspired choice.

Berlin announced, "I've decided not to go back to Hollywood, but to stay in the theater regardless of what happens to *Annie*. What I really want to do next is another *Music Box Revue*."

But post-war audiences were ready for *Annie*—just as much as Annie was ready for them. It was destined to be his biggest Broadway success in years. The *Music Box Revue* was from a different generation. It took a lot of persuading to convince Berlin of this. He never came completely to terms with this fact, but in the later forties things were going so well for him it no longer mattered.

He certainly didn't want to go back to Hollywood. "I wrote *Holiday Inn* in 1941 and it wasn't until 1942 or later that people saw it. All that time the songs are hidden away and you have no way of knowing whether they'll be accepted or rejected. Or maybe even duplicated."

"When you do a picture score," he told reporters as *Annie* was getting ready for its first performance, "you may find that one of your best has been killed by something someone else wrote in the meantime. The Hollywood yardstick for success," he said, "is business. At the end of the year, perhaps longer, they'll tell you how much gross business your picture did and then you'll know whether it is a success or not. With a Broadway show you get the bad news or the good right away. You don't have to wait. And you get to hear people singing your songs right away, too, which is very pleasant."

The *New York Herald Tribune* commented, "Facing the opening of *Annie Get Your Gun*, Mr. Berlin has all his fingers crossed including the magic one with which he is falsely accused of writing all his music. But he is happier than most showmen when they prepare to walk the last mile between 'tryout and findout.' He is coming back to Broadway and that, he says, is good enough."

Annie had nineteen brand-new numbers in it. He hadn't used his filing cabinet once. When the show opened on Broadway, the *Herald Tribune* headlined its review, "Bull's Eye." As with every other writer, it was the music which impressed the paper's critic most. He wrote, "Irving Berlin's songs form a fascinating web of wit and melody for the action."

In all, on this first time around, *Annie* ran for a total of 1,147 performances; overseas tours and U.S. touring companies added to the total.

The same year that people whistled and sang numbers like "The Sun in the Morning" and "There's No Business Like Show Business," Ellin received a check for $60,000, her current royalties from "Always."

Berlin won the Donaldson Award for the best score of the year with *Annie,* Ethel Merman got the Donaldson for the best performance, and Joshua Logan received another for the best direction.

Berlin was also awarded the Roosevelt Medal, presented jointly to him and to Generals Eisenhower and MacArthur and Admirals Nimitz and Halsey. He was introduced as "an American by choice, a patriot who shares with his countrymen his gifts, his time, his energy and his earnings, and a singer whose songs warm the hearts of 140 million Americans." As usual, Berlin thanked the assembled dignitaries from a piano, and the performance ended with a chorus of "God Bless America" for which the assembled company stood and spontaneously joined in.

The National Conference of Christians and Jews also honored him that year, together with Spyros P. Skouras and Robert E. Sherwood, "for the contributions they have made in the world of the theater and advancing the aims of the conference to eliminate religious and racial conflict."

The award to Berlin was made by James A. Farley, the former Democratic Party National Chairman. "No one really knows how much inspiration his songs gave to the people who carry them in their hearts, but he has also given the citizens of America a personal interest in the human aspects of their citizen armies by writing two army shows for two World Wars." As a gesture of thanks in return, Berlin wrote "Help Me to Help My Neighbor."

Not everyone was being as neighborly as Berlin might have hoped. In 1946 he was back in the courts, this time not complaining about parodies of his songs, but requesting damages and an injunction against the Universal Writers of America, an organization which he said had been soliciting ten-dollar memberships through the unjustified use of his name.

Ellin still had writing and politics to give time to. She had supported Newbold Morris as an independent candidate for Mayor of New York back in 1945. "I have three daughters and am interested in keeping New York a clean, happy place for children to grow up in. Other mothers feel the way I do. We don't want to give our city back to Tammany." Despite Morris's defeat, she retained her social conscience.

She was also working on a novel that was said to be more than a little bit autobiographical. But publication was to wait till Irving got back from Hollywood.

For although he had committed his heart to Broadway, there had been an irresistible offer from the film capital. MGM offered him $500,000 for *Easter Parade*, yet another potpourri of the old and the best Berlin tunes. It was to star Judy Garland, Frank Sinatra, Kathryn Grayson, Red Skelton, and Gene Kelly. There was also Peter Lawford and Ann Miller. Sinatra, Grayson, and Skelton left before contracts could be signed and Gene Kelly broke a leg, so the main dance part went to Fred Astaire. With Astaire and Judy Garland teamed to sing and dance, Irving Berlin's music couldn't fail.

Here was a chance for Berlin to make a lot of money, as usual, through percentages. Rumor was that his cut was going to be worth not $500,000 but $600,000. But it was all conjecture. Irving insisted that any money from his film had to come from a healthy slice of what was taken at the box office.

Twentieth Century-Fox had been first to come up with the

idea of *Easter Parade*. But they weren't interested in percentages, so Berlin told them he wasn't interested in the new film.

It had been settled, so he thought, when he and Joseph M. Schenck, then head of Twentieth Century-Fox, came to an informal understanding.

Schenck's executives had discussed the matter at length and then sent off a long wire which amounted to: SORRY NO DEAL STOP BUT CAN OFFER YOU SOMETHING TO BRING IN MUCH MORE.

Berlin apologized for being awkward, but said it was a matter of principle. He got a percentage or nothing.

Louis B. Mayer then said he would offer more than Twentieth Century-Fox if Berlin would agree to work on the film at his MGM studio, but still there would be no percentage. To which Berlin answered, "Why should I ask one thing from Schenck and another from you?"

Mayer allowed Berlin to win, MGM made *Easter Parade*, and audiences all over the world could again enjoy "When That Midnight Choo-Choo Leaves for Alabam," "The Girl on the Magazine Cover," and "Easter Parade" itself. The old songs blended easily with the new which included "A Feller with an Umbrella," "It Only Happens When I Dance with You," "Steppin' Out with My Baby," and the funniest and one of the nicest he ever wrote, "A Couple of Swells." And Berlin got his percentage.

It was the last number that brought the house down wherever the movie played. Berlin had come into the MGM studio one day and said simply: "Let's have a 'tramps' number." No one could think of any reason why not. So a tramps number there was, with Judy and Fred, teeth blacked out, evening dress and tails tattered, laughing as they walked up the avenue because they didn't have the fare to travel any other way.

Everyone was good in *Easter Parade*, perhaps because, as Astaire said at the time, they realized "this has no purpose but to divert the audiences with Berlin's music." After taxes, Berlin earned $640,000 in 1947.

Much of Berlin's success as a songwriter was due to the sudden renascence after the war of the phonograph record. It had seemed to be the principal loser when the talkies came in, and when radio became as big as it did it looked like the end of the road. Some of the biggest stars, like Al Jolson, had stopped recording altogether during the 1930s. But by 1948, it was big business again.

Then something happened to threaten this vital cog of the music machine. Musicians went on strike because they intended to force theaters, restaurants, and most important, radio stations to employ live musicians rather than rely on shellac disks.

The strike began on January 1, 1948. No orchestras would be available to play for records. The stars who wanted to continue to cut records would have to sing without accompaniment, or, if they were lucky, to find groups like the Mills Brothers who were constantly busy because they had their own guitar accompaniment.

But it wasn't easy on Berlin who couldn't guarantee just when an idea for a song would hit him. So he was really faced with a tremendous problem when on December 31, 1947, he had an idea that he knew would make him a lot of money.

He was in Mexico for Christmas and came up with a number called "In Acapulco" which he knew would be what people wanted to hear, especially if they were going to be starved of other tunes in the months to come.

Still in Mexico, Berlin phoned his New York office, got his musical secretary, and croaked out the words and the music of the new number. With barely hours to spare, the music was rushed, fully orchestrated, to Guy Lombardo who recorded it with his Royal Canadians just before the ban by the American Federation of Musicians came into force. It was no great song, but people bought it just as Berlin had known they would.

To set some other record, Berlin was awarded France's Legion of Honor Cross of Knighthood. The French Consul kissed Berlin on the cheeks during the presentation, of course. "So many of your songs have been translated into French, Monsieur Berlin," he said.

That was no surprise to Berlin. For years he'd been receiving those royalty checks that came in from France.

Irving Berlin's own voice was still raspy and high-pitched, but he could sometimes be persuaded to go on radio shows. It was always a chance to bring in more Berlin royalties.

On one show with Bing Crosby and Al Jolson, Berlin had just satisfied himself with a rendition of "Oh, How I Hate to Get Up in the Morning" when Jolson chimed in. "Irving, I know you have a reputation for never lifting a tune," he said. "But I never knew till tonight that you couldn't carry one, either."

Then he reminded Berlin smugly that he had just written a tune himself, the current hit, "The Anniversary Song."

"The melody is very familiar," said Berlin. "Even I remember it. It's over a hundred years old."

"You *should* remember it," said Jolson.

Then Bing Crosby interrupted to tell Berlin, "I've something to confess to you that I've been wanting to tell you for a long time. The first song I ever mangled in a picture was written by you."

"Well, Bing," Berlin replied. "I've something to confess to *you*. I really can't remember which song or which picture you're talking about."

Indeed, Berlin had written so many songs by then that, as he said once, "I can hear a song that I wrote forty or fifty years ago and have completely forgotten. But then I get an old copy out and look at the lyrics and it comes back to me."

As a tribute to his own sense of "remember when?" Irving took Ellin on a trip around the old Chinatown and Bowery he'd known. It was 1947.

"It's like going home after being away so many years," he told her as they walked the streets. They stopped at the doorway of Number 12 Pell Street—where "Nigger" Mike had had his saloon and where Irving had written "Marie from Sunny Italy" all those years before. "I was paid seven dollars a week here," he told Ellin, for whom seven dollars had never represented much more than the price of a hat. They stopped briefly to listen to an evangelist conducting services for the neighborhood's down-and-outs, and bumped into Jimmy Kelly, the former fighter who had once been Berlin's employer. "You were a darn good boss, Jim," Berlin told him.

Then they took a bus tour of the Bowery. The guide stopped off at 12 Pell Street and talked about Irving Berlin.

"He's got all the facts wrong," Irving told Ellin. "It sounds like a movie scenario."

Just then, Berlin spotted someone he hadn't seen since he'd been a singing waiter. "Hello, Izzy," said the old-timer. "That guide's giving out a lot of baloney. Do you think I ought to biff him?"

Berlin slipped the man a ten-dollar bill and asked him not to say anything. "His heart's in the right place," said Berlin.

In June 1948, America celebrated forty years of Irving Berlin's writing songs for the country with a Berlin Week. The American Federation of Radio Artists immediately asked him to join the union. "You're supplying more music and being played more than any other artist," an official told him. The Berlin Week turned out rather more happily than when the Boy Scouts decided to honor him.

For his contribution to Scouting in the hundreds of thousands of dollars they had earned from the proceeds of "God Bless America," the Scouts decided it was only right to give him one of their highest awards, the Silver Buffalo. Unfortunately, the man who was in charge of musical arrangements for the evening had not done his homework. Berlin was welcomed to the ceremony and invited to sit back and enjoy his music. So for thirty minutes, Berlin, the Scouts, and their families were treated to the best of Jerome Kern. But Irving didn't complain.

Later that year, Rodgers and Hammerstein established a scholarship for composition in his name at New York's Juilliard School of Music. It was to be available to any city public school graduate. That, they knew, was a scholarship very close to Berlin's heart, giving the people with music in their blood the "science" he'd never had.

Berlin was now sixty, an age in life when most people begin looking for carpet slippers. But not Berlin. He did a little fishing in the stream that ran through his Catskills farm, but it was mainly a place to hum out ideas for new songs. He played golf a little, but it never held his interest for long.

His biggest problem was insomnia. Once brought on by the need to compose at night, it was now a constant problem. As he got older, the problem worsened. His friends and family knew it was not to be mentioned more than necessary in his company. On one occasion, a friend seemed pleasantly surprised when Berlin surfaced comparatively early in the day, looking as smart and dapper as ever, his still black curly hair neatly combed in place.

"Why, Irving, you look as if you slept well last night!" said the friend.

"Yeah," Berlin agreed grudgingly, "but I dreamed that I didn't."

The pretty Berlin daughters were growing up. In July 1948 the society columns of the newspapers were happier about an event in the family than they had been since the elopement in 1926.

Mary Ellin, the Berlins' eldest daughter, was married at their New York home to Dennis S. Burden. Only close family was present at the ceremony and the bride's sisters, Linda Louise and Elizabeth Irving, were the only attendants.

Show business marriages had crumbled all around them over the years, and Irving and Ellin were justifiably proud of the success of their own. They felt they stood as a good example to Mary Ellin and Dennis that day when the Rev. George B. Ford conducted the service.

After the ceremony, Rabbi Morris Lazaron, a friend of Berlin's, gave a special blessing. In many ways it was Berlin's assertion that he still owed something to his own roots, even though his children had been brought up as Christians.

Despite his wartime bipartisanship in national elections, Berlin was at heart a Republican. In July 1948, he wrote a song that he didn't think would ever be published, one that supported General Eisenhower as a Republican presidential candidate. Before long, Thomas Dewey was nominated and Truman was re-elected, but Berlin just quietly put aside his song idea.

When next he came to London, the *Star* noted that Berlin looked "worried," and that "his voice rasped like a detuned radio." Business associates were quick to assure the newspaper that his "worry" was simply that he had "another world-beater of a tune in his mind."

Berlin then denied it and pointed to the fact that for the first time there was no piano in his suite at Claridge's. This time he was there as Berlin the businessman. Two years before, he had opened his own London office, Irving Berlin Ltd., in Hanover Square. Now he was in town to try systematically to buy back all his old copyrights as he had done almost everywhere else. "I want to publish my old ones as well as the new," he said, and began business in Britain with "You Keep Coming Back Like a Song."

Not for the first time, was he asked to spell out his recipe for writing successful songs. "Songs do well," he said, "if they are based on one of these ideas: first, home; second, love; third, self-pity—you know like 'What'll I Do?' or 'All Alone'—and fourth, happiness."

He said he had six favorite songs, but wouldn't care to name them. They were all by Irving Berlin. They were probably Ellin's favorites, too. She made no secret of the fact that she liked his songs better than anyone else's and he did as much to plug her books as he did to get people to buy his songs.

When *The Lace Curtain* came out, the publishers made a big play out of the fact that it was about a mixed marriage, one between a Catholic and a Protestant. Berlin was ready to answer the inevitable reporters' questions; "That was not our problem," he told them. He was not a Protestant. "But I think the book *is* largely autobiographical." Offers for the stage and film rights to the "true" Berlin story came cascading in, but the answer to each was always no.

He was now interested in doing a show which he had provisionally entitled *Stars on My Shoulder,* about a forgotten general who tries to get a job in peacetime. When Berlin came to London to see their version of *Annie Get Your Gun,* starring Dolores Gray in the Merman part, Emile Littler tried to tie him down to doing a new London musical. Berlin suggested *Stars on My Shoulder* but the suggestion wasn't taken up.

The London Palladium, where Berlin had scored such a hit with *This Is the Army* six years before, had become a showplace for big stars from the States. Danny Kaye had made an enormous hit there, and in August 1948, it was the Andrews Sisters who were rocking people in the aisles.

Halfway through their act one night, Patti Andrews went to the footlights and said, "There is a man in the audience I'd like to have you meet." She threw out her arms in a welcome and Irving Berlin stood up, walked down the center aisle, and then climbed on to the stage.

In the spotlight he blinked, croaked "Alexander's Ragtime Band," and brought the house down. The audience knew who he was without his being introduced. Then he did a dance with Patti.

After the show, Emile Littler again suggested a new show from Berlin. Val Parnell, the Palladium chief, added he would back it sight unseen. Now, however, Berlin was being a little cagey. "I'll think it over," he said.

The press had been impressed with his impromptu Palladium performance. "At sixty," one man reported, "Irving Berlin looks like an amiable gremlin—all grin and glasses."

Others were less kind. "He's much more interested in commercial success than artistic quality," said one. Berlin bristled. "A little Van Gogh painting may cost ten thousand pounds," he said. "Would you say *that* was a purely commercial item?"

By Christmas Berlin was in Germany with Bob Hope on one of

that entertainer's first post-war expeditions to the troops. When he finally got back, Berlin did what everybody expected. He wrote a new song called "Oh, to Be Home Again." And home it seemed again in March 1949, when the Young Men's Hebrew Association in New York celebrated its 75th anniversary as America's oldest and largest community center by giving him an Award of Merit. He was one of twelve men chosen as "Outstanding Americans of the Jewish Faith."

His trip to London had given Berlin the itch to get on with a new musical and he thought he now had the idea for one that London would buy as eagerly as would Broadway. But he was wrong.

19

The Hostess with the Mostest

ROBERT E. SHERWOOD, THE famed playwright who had once worked on President Roosevelt's staff and had written the celebrated book about the Roosevelt-Hopkins partnership, now had a different idea: to write a Broadway musical. He put the plan to Berlin while they were both in Britain. "It's an idea that's right up your alley, Irving," Sherwood told him. "A musical about the Statue of Liberty."

Sherwood said the idea had come to him while sailing into New York on a troopship. The effect on the military passengers must have been similar to the impact it had on boatloads of immigrants who had steamed into New York harbor at the turn of the century, immigrants like the Balines.

Over dinner together a couple of nights later, Sherwood's conviction suddenly took root in Berlin's mind, too. The men were ordering from the menu when Berlin started humming a few bars of a melody and scribbling down some words for a lyric. He wasn't very good dinner company thereafter.

Back in this country and back at the Buick he sat smoking pack after pack, chewing gum as he puffed and plunked away.

Sherwood was doing the play, but Berlin got intensely involved in the story, too, doing what research he could on the side. It was the beginning of a constant collaboration. The two men consulted each other on the minutest detail.

182

Within five months they had a score, a book, and a title: *Miss Liberty*.

At the first rehearsal at Berlin's own theatre, The Music Box, Berlin played through the whole score and the cast clapped loudly. It was Berlin's twentieth show and he was determined to make it a good score's worth. As he confessed to the people at The Music Box that day, "I'll be happy with a good old-fashioned commercial smash hit."

But he had pushed himself a little too hard. For the first time in his career he tried something almost symphonic as accompaniment to Emma Lazarus's famous inscription on the plinth of the statue, "Give me your tired, your poor . . ."

There were also Berlin words and music for "The Most Expensive Statue in the World," "Falling in Love Can Be Fun," "Paris Wakes Up and Smiles," "Just One Way to Say I Love You," and the charming "Let's Take an Old-Fashioned Walk."

At one rehearsal, Moss Hart, who was never renowned for his musical ear, dropped in and asked Berlin to play one of the new *Miss Liberty* numbers.

Berlin obliged on the standard piano in the theater. Hart didn't know whether to complain or keep quiet. "Play 'Always,' " he shouted. Berlin again obliged. To Hart, it sounded exactly the same as the previous number had: terrible. But he clapped loudly at the tinny sounds, and said it would fit in fine with the rest of the score, oblivious to the fact that Berlin had just played a twenty-three-year-old tune.

In June 1949, the whole cast with principals Eddie Albert and Mary McCarty, moved to Philadelphia for the opening.

The press liked *Miss Liberty* in Philadelphia and the audience cheered, but Berlin himself knew that all was not well.

For the Broadway opening, critical knives had been sharpened. Brooks Atkinson, in the *New York Times:* "To come right out and say it, *Miss Liberty* is a disappointing musical comedy put together without sparkle or originality." He did manage to predict, "No doubt everyone in America will be familiar soon with

'Let's Take an Old-Fashioned Walk,' simple and sweet in tune."

They were indeed. But they were never to become familiar with *Miss Liberty* herself. The show died within a few months. It never got the London opening Berlin had wanted so much, despite the offer of a blank check from Emile Littler and Val Parnell.

It was galling for Berlin to read the critics. Brooks Atkinson followed up his original review with another piece in the paper's Sunday edition. Adding insult to injury, he called *Miss Liberty* a "mediocre musical" which had been "done to a worn formula without imagination or originality. Given Robert E. Sherwood, Irving Berlin, and Moss Hart, a cautious theatre goer is likely to expect something with spirit and flavor."

Atkinson said of Berlin: "His style and spirit fit the American idiom perfectly." But they didn't fit this show. He liked Mary McCarty and said, "If Mr. Sherwood and Mr. Berlin wrote with as much vitality as she acts, *Miss Liberty* might not be such a commonplace show. From every point of view the Statue of Liberty is a happy subject for them. But they have not written it.

"Bogged down in the cliches of old-fashioned musical comedy, they have not even written about the grand lady who holds the torch over our harbor. In view of their special gifts as writers, they have missed the opportunity of their Broadway careers."

After forty years of songwriting, Irving Berlin had never seen such criticism of his songs, one or two of which Atkinson conceded did "something towards redeeming the general mediocrity of the show."

Berlin was bitter and at sixty-two he felt washed up. And he was even tentatively admitting it. "I've never been in a tougher spot than I'm in right now," he admitted in a rare moment of candor to Ward Morehouse in the *New York Sun,* early in 1950. "Talent is only the starting point in this business," he told Morehouse. "You've got to keep on working at it. And some day I'll reach for it, and it won't be there."

As always, nothing cheered him up more than feeling he could give as much as he felt he had received. "God Bless America" had earned such vast sums for the Scouts that he now made a gift of his new *Miss Liberty* song, "Give Me Your Tired," to a fund which would support nonsectarian, nonracial organizations.

Then the sudden prospect of activities of his own cheered him further. On his way to a short holiday in Europe with Ellin and their daughters Linda and Elizabeth, he revealed that he had signed for a new musical based on the life of Mrs. Perle Mesta. She was the American society figure who had just been named by President Truman as his Ambassador to Luxembourg.

It was supposed to be fictional, but it did happen to be about a society woman going to a tiny Grand Duchy in Europe as Ambassador for a man she called "Harry" several times in the show. Her previous reputation had been as a famous party giver in White House circles.

"Does Mrs. Mesta know about this show, Mr. Berlin?"

"I don't know," he replied. "But she'll know about it soon enough, with Ethel Merman in the lead."

It was a good score, and Berlin knew it. RCA announced they were sponsoring the show to the tune of the $250,000 needed to produce it. To which the *New York Times* commented drily that Ethel Merman's lyrics would surely have to be punctuated by occasional RCA commercials.

However, when *Call Me Madam* opened for a tryout in New Haven, Conn., the only sound between Merman's songs was the audience's clapping and cheers.

The second act wasn't nearly so perfect as the first. "It needs something else to lift it," said Merman. "It needs something more."

"You're right," Berlin agreed. He stayed up all night, paced the floor, burned more holes in the Buick's ivories, and next day presented Ethel with the answer to their problem.

A duet called "You're Just in Love." It was all the show could possibly have needed.

New York Times critic Brooks Atkinson said that *"Call Me Madam* ought to give thousands pleasure. After forty-five years on the sidewalks of Tin Pan Alley, Mr. Berlin is entitled to lose some of his rapture and enthusiasm. He doesn't. He has bestowed on *Call Me Madam* one of his most delightful cornucopias of sound." Berlin hardly needed to read further. But Mr. Atkinson continued,

To a theatregoer who first became aware of Mr. Berlin's special brand of genius amid the dismal sandstorms of *Yaphank* in 1918, his longevity as a composer is not only amazing but gratifying. The music of *Call Me Madam* is cheerful and intimate and the lyrics are effortless and amusing. Over the years, Mr. Berlin has probably written a number of songs in the casual vein of "It's a Lovely Day Today," but none of them has been more enchanting.

No doubt, Mr. Berlin keeps fresh from generation to generation by taking an interest in the people and maintaining a sympathetic interest in the times. He has long since mastered the American idiom. But instead of exploiting it, he serves it sincerely.

To no one's surprise, Perle Mesta not only heard about the show but went to see it with Bess Truman and the President's daughter Margaret. All of them called on Ethel Merman in her dressing room later and said they'd enjoyed the spoof immensely.

"It's nice to have a hit again in *Call Me Madam*," Berlin told reporters in London late in 1950. "It's wonderful at my age to reach for success and find it's still there."

Success still spelled money, of course. For a one-hour television show in 1951, Berlin got about $40,000 for a performance with another celebrated musician, Margaret Truman. Proceeds were donated to the Boy Scouts and Girl Scouts of America.

However friendly he was to the Truman family, Berlin's political sentiments lay elsewhere. One of the songs in *Call Me Madam* directly reflected his feelings about the presidential election coming up in 1952. It was called simply "They Like Ike." Sure enough, the title was adapted by the Republicans to become the best-known political slogan of all time, "I Like Ike." The Eisenhower-for-President campaign got underway with a monster rally at New York's Madison Square Garden. Theme song for the occasion was the Berlin tune, which ended with the line, "Even Harry Truman Says 'I Like Ike.' "

Call Me Madam was as much of a sensation in London as it was in New York. Said the *Manchester Guardian:* "*Call Me Madam* had a friendly, indeed almost fanatical reception at the Coliseum last night." Berlin himself had chosen actress Billie Worth for the Ethel Merman part and everyone agreed that the choice was delightful.

Surprisingly, Ellin Berlin was now actively working for Eisenhower's election. She had been one of a couple dozen signers of a letter to newspapers which said, "Independent of any restraints imposed by partisan interests, and placing the welfare of our country above party loyalty, we call for the election of General Eisenhower. Peace and security are the most important issues facing the American people."

For Ellin and Irving both, world peace was of paramount interest. But there were problems of family strife for them to face as well. Mary Ellin had divorced her husband and had married a Californian named Marvin Barrett. Devoted parents, the Berlins had been worried about the girl's happiness.

Berlin showed his interest in other people's children too, by endowing a $15,000 music scholarship at Bucknell University. What gave him special pleasure was that his generosity followed one of his own most important accolades. Bucknell had awarded Berlin, who still couldn't read a note of music, an honorary doctorate—of music.

20

I'm Sorry for Myself

THE FIRM OF IRVING BERLIN Inc. didn't need the money that the success of *Call Me Madam* was producing. One version after another of "You're Just in Love" and "It's a Lovely Day Today" was recorded, bought, and played. Irving Berlin himself didn't need the money. But he did need the satisfaction that only hit songs could bring. The businessman inside his hit factory had always enjoyed hearing the cash register jingle when songs by other people on his list did well, but the songwriter was always a bit jealous.

"How could he be satisfied when he only gets the publisher's royalties?" joked one cynic. "He needs to scoop up the composer's and the lyricist's too." That was only part of the answer. The rest was pride.

Criticism of any of his work in the last few years had made him retreat and worry. But now he was on top again. Even Perle Mesta had adopted one of his songs for the show, "The Hostess with the Mostest," as her personal slogan.

He could take jokes about himself again. There was one going the rounds in New York. With a growing reputation as a gourmet, Berlin enjoyed more than anything a good meal at the Colony or some other really good Manhattan restaurant.

At one particular place he and the *maître d'hôtel* had become particularly friendly. Berlin trusted the other's judgment implicitly and always ordered whatever was suggested or pointed out on the menu.

One evening after a fine meal, Berlin thanked the *maître d'* and mentioned that he expected to be out of town for some time. "Very good, sir," said the *maître d'*. "If you have any friends who can't read either, tell them to ask for me, too."

In London, he was blatantly asked about being a millionaire. "Look," he said, "everyone must make money to live. But I do not write only for money. That just comes."

It was true that the songs which gave him the greatest pride were those on which he had not made a cent himself. In 1954, nine-year-old Doris Lewis was presented with the Bronze Cross of the American Girl Scouts for rescuing her two younger sisters and waking up her parents when their house caught fire. At the ceremony she was introduced to Berlin who promptly sang "God Bless America" to her instead of making the speech that he had been expected to deliver.

On another medal-giving occasion that year, Berlin did make a brief speech. At the suggestion of General Eisenhower, Congress passed a special appropriation for $1,500, the cost of striking a new medal. It was going to Irving Berlin. On a bright sunny day in July 1954, Irving and Ellin were received at the White House by their friend the President. Smiling broadly for photographers, Ike gave Irving first his award and then the Bill which had authorized him to have the special gold medal struck, "in recognition of his services in composing many popular songs, including 'God Bless America.' "

After the ceremony, Berlin was asked what the President had said to him. "I can't tell you," he said in a voice even more hoarse than usual. "I'm so emotionally filled up, I don't remember."

The day after the ceremony, the *New York Times* thought the occasion important enough to write an editorial about Berlin and his medal:

Irving Berlin's early life in this country was simple indeed. But his East Side beginnings were not wasted. They gave him a feeling for the hopes and fears of the men in the street.

Out of his early struggles came one of the first broken rhythm classics, "Alexander's Ragtime Band."

Out of his gratitude to the country which gave him so many opportunities came "God Bless America." Strangely enough Mr. Berlin didn't think this song good enough to keep in a revue he wrote for the Army in 1917. It wasn't brought out until 1938. It has stayed out since.

Irving Berlin has not only given the public music that it loved, he has also given his time and his talents in two wars. All the royalties of "God Bless America," and they have been considerable, go to a trust fund for the Girl Scouts and Boy Scouts of America. Every penny of the proceeds of *This Is the Army* produced in 1942 went to the Army Emergency Relief.

For these and other reasons, there couldn't be a more popular law than the one that now gives Mr. Berlin his medal. May he wear it for many years to come.

In the early 1950s, he was sleeping worse than ever. He had tried everything, even counting sheep. "Try counting your blessings instead," said Ellin and so helped him to produce another song.

It was featured in the 1954 movie, *White Christmas*. A song like *that* one had to have a movie built around it. Paramount brought in Bing Crosby, Danny Kaye, and Rosemary Clooney for a suitable romantic story about war-time troop entertaining and what had heppened to the artists after the war.

The film was another opportunity for a potpourri of Berlin standards ranging from "White Christmas" back to "Mandy" and "Blue Skies," to a string of new ones. There was "The Best Things Happen When You're Dancing," which would have delighted Fred Astaire, who was originally going to star with Crosby but who had to withdraw because of illness. Rosemary Clooney and Vera-Ellen had a very funny number called "Sisters" and the entire cast put its ironic heart into "Gee, I Wish I Was Back in the Army."

The best newcomer, though, was "Count Your Blessings Instead of Sheep," which immediately became a best seller.

Eddie Fisher, singing sensation of the decade, sang it in 1954 at a banquet to mark the tercentenary of the settlement of America's Jews. Fisher told the gathering that Berlin had asked that the number be dedicated "to our greatest blessing, our President."

The 1954 Christopher Award for achievements in radio, television, motion pictures and songwriting went to Berlin for "Count Your Blessings" because he had shown he was a man who "used his God-given talents for the benefit of all."

The movie was largely responsible for boosting his 1955 royalties for "White Christmas" to a million dollars in one year alone.

A filmed version of *Annie Get Your Gun,* starring Betty Hutton, was still going the rounds and the few Judy Garland recordings from the soundtrack—she had been "relieved" from the picture after her attempted suicide—were avidly sought by fans.

The *Call Me Madam* film looked set for being an even greater success than the Broadway original. Ethel Merman was again in the lead, backed this time by the always popular Donald O'Connor and the suave as ever George Sanders.

Another Berlin film finished the 1954 season. *There's No Business Like Show Business* resurrected the "anthem" from *Annie Get Your Gun* and included such Berlin songs as "Remember," "A Pretty Girl Is Like a Melody," "Alexander's Ragtime Band," and "You'd Be Surprised." But the sensation of the film was Berlin's beautiful "Lazy," sung by a magnificently beautiful Marilyn Monroe.

When Berlin heard that the Boy Scouts wanted a new camp site at Staten Island, he wrote a check to cover it. And a little later, he pledged ten thousand dollars toward another cause close to his heart. He heard that a statue was planned in honor of the man who had meant so much to him in his early years, George M. Cohan, and that it was going to be put in the heart of Broadway. Berlin couldn't resist helping to honor the man who had done so much for him a generation before.

Irving Berlin still gave the impression of looking younger than his years, his hair gleaming with a shine that betrayed barely a touch of gray, and of seeming happier than he had been for years. He wasn't. In fact, he could have won a diploma for depression for he had decided to try concentrating on the hardest job of all, retirement.

He started to paint and only got morose because he wasn't as good a painter as a songwriter. He did a little fishing, but what he was really fishing for in the waters around his Catskills farm were new songs. Yet, as he waded into the streams, new ideas didn't bite any more readily than real fish.

He played a little golf, but if songs came to his mind they were there for fleeting seconds and disappeared more readily than golf balls.

He and Ellin tried to get away from his problem of worrying about nothing by taking long vacations, but they rarely helped. One Christmas they were in Haiti, staying at a luxury hotel there. Irving, feeling more down than ever, sat with Ellin by the open-air bar near the swimming pool. He brightened for a moment or two when Noel Coward came up to them and introduced a party of friends.

Coward brought Paris couturier Ginette Spanier in his party, and she was delighted to meet a songwriter she had admired for so long. "He seemed to me at that time to be a little old man who was feeling very, very sad," she said later.

Once he had exchanged pleasantries with Coward and his friends, Berlin felt it was safe to stop smiling again. But then he heard the sound of a piano tinkling a few yards away. It was "White Christmas" being played on the bar's upright piano. The pianist then gave his interpretation of "Easter Parade," followed by another tune. Berlin turned and recognized the pianist. It was Noel Coward.

He went up to Coward after a little while to compliment him on his playing. "Who wrote that tune?" he asked.

"You did," said Coward. It had been so long that Berlin had forgotten one of his own melodies.

The afternoon turned to evening and the bar filled with guests, as many as could crowd around the piano. Some of them begged Coward to play one of his own songs.

"No," he told them. "This is Irving Berlin's night." And he went on playing one Berlin number after another.

When he had finished, Berlin was smiling a wider smile than anyone had seen for months. There was joy in Ellin's eyes too, reflected, perhaps, in the pearl necklace she wore that day. The pearls were the famous Mackay pearls once owned by her grandmother. She led Irving toward Coward amid everyone's cheers. By the time they reached the piano, Ellin had her arms out wide and then she planted a big kiss on Coward's cheek.

"Noel, darling," she smiled. "You'll never know what you have done for Irving today."

The trouble with Berlin was that he had never learned how to relax without working.

"I never had a hobby," he often said. "Songwriting was my hobby." He was happy at times such as those evenings in Haiti, hearing his music played. He was happier still when he was creating something good on his own Buick. He always had to be the busiest and best songwriter around.

He even demonstrated his abilities once in the New York State Supreme Court when Justice Martin M. Frank was asked to determine whether or not Berlin had stolen "You're Just in Love," from *Call Me Madam*, from a part-time composer named Joseph Smith.

Smith was a fifty-three-year-old gold stamper by trade who claimed he had written a song called "I Fell in Love." He had then

handed it to a man named Willie Moskowitz, whom he believed to
be an employee of Berlin's music publishing firm.

Like Berlin, Smith could neither read nor write music.

The gold stamper had brought a lawyer, a pianist, and a piano
into the courtroom. He testified that he had written "I Fell in
Love" in 1947. As an expert witness, he produced Abram Chasins,
the musical director for radio station WQXR, who went to the
piano and picked out Mr. Smith's melody.

When the moment came for cross-examination, Berlin's at-
torney Monroe Goldwater stepped to the piano and himself sang
Berlin's song while Mr. Chasins played.

Chasins told the court, "Mr. Goldwater is a very musical man
for a lawyer. His baritone is what could be called a parlor voice
with a kitchen range." The two tunes, he testified, were identical.

The *New York Times* reported that the courtroom "sounded
like a cross between an old-fashioned barber shop and Tin Pan
Alley." But it agreed that when Berlin took the stand, the court
was treated to a "musical bonus."

The song was his, Berlin said. He had written it in a hurry in
New Haven, Conn., because both he and Ethel Merman, as well as
director George Abbott, felt that it was needed for the second part
of *Call Me Madam.*

Berlin admitted that the germ of the song was not necessarily
new, but said it was his own. He had a storehouse of memories of
old songs and for this he had dug up an idea he'd played around
with before World War I.

"I'll demonstrate how I worked," said Berlin. And without the
help of a lever he tapped out "You're Just in Love" on the courtroom piano. It was a performance he thoroughly enjoyed, as did
everyone else in court.

In a seventeen-page document, Judge Frank declared Irving
Berlin the winner on points. He said the evidence had been "quite
to the contrary" that Berlin and his corporation had access to
Smith's music and that he was satisfied that no Willie Moskowitz

had worked for Berlin's firm or that the songwriter had ever known anyone by that name.

Berlin had won his case. He had no real worries, but for years he worried and for years he felt ill. All because he wasn't composing steadily anymore.

He continued to paint. Then in 1957 he wrote a song which Rosemary Clooney recorded called "You Can't Lose the Blues with Colors." The year before, he had failed to console himself with a number called "Anybody Can Write."

Occasionally, he would come out of retirement, but not really for the sort of show business performance that might have done him good. One of these occasions was another opportunity to honor Eisenhower. In 1956 Berlin led the Republican National Convention in the singing of his campaign song, "Ike for Four More Years," based on "Three Blind Mice."

If he wrote other new songs, they were generally for personal reasons. "Silver Platter," went with Ellin's new biography of her grandmother, and songs for his grandchildren used their names as titles, "Irving Berlin Barrett" and "Song for Elizabeth Esther Barrett."

In 1953, he had written a tune called "Sayonara, Sayonara" but had stored it away. Four years later he brought it out again (the last Berlin movie theme to date) to go with the Marlon Brando film *Sayonara*. Once again, Eddie Fisher recorded it and once again, after that brief moment of glory, Berlin became depressed.

In 1958, for the first time in fifty years, not a single new Berlin tune was copyrighted. Friends told him to relax and enjoy himself. He couldn't.

Nor would he allow people to pay what they considered to be just tributes to him. Movie companies still begged him to allow them to make films of his life. He turned them down each time. "There's only been one biographical movie of a songwriter that hasn't made me too embarrassed to sit and watch it, and that was

George M. Cohan's *Yankee Doodle Dandy,"* he told me. "I couldn't take the risk of one about me turning out to be a syrupy tribute."

He was offered hundreds of thousands of dollars to write an autobiography or agree to an authorized biography. He said no.

For his seventieth birthday in May 1958, the BBC decided to pay tribute to Berlin with a televised biography. Gaylord Cavallaro, who looked uncannily like Berlin when sitting at a piano keyboard with his hair slicked down, was signed to play the lead.

The trouble was, as producer Ernest Maxim admitted three days before transmission, no one had bothered to tell Berlin about the plans. So three days before transmission the whole thing had to be changed. The BBC could play his music but no one could play Berlin's part. Maxim phoned Berlin's office in New York but they were insistent.

Still no one bothered to tell Berlin himself. But his office would not allow the show to go ahead. Miss Hilda Schneider, who is still Berlin's secretary, said, "He is such a shy and retiring man that he shuns all kind of publicity. He has refused vast fortunes to let Hollywood do his life story or American TV to present it as a spectacular.

"How would it have looked if suddenly it popped up in Britain? No one there bothered to ask his permission. If they had asked, they would have saved themselves a lot of trouble."

"We are so sure of ourselves," she added, "that we haven't even bothered to tell him what we have done."

Later, when Berlin did hear about it, he said, "I don't want my life story told. It would be an invasion of my privacy while I'm still alive. When I'm dead they can tell it all they want."

Berlin was always generous about other people's music. When *My Fair Lady* broke all records, he said it was the best show he had ever seen. "You don't have to be different to be good," he said. "And if you're good, you are different." A pure Berlinism. What he didn't add was that in 1951, soon after George Bernard Shaw's death, the playwright's executors had approached Berlin and asked if he would be interested in doing a musical based on *Pygmalion.* Berlin had said he was too heavily committed and let the idea slide.

Now he often thought how much he would like to do a new show of his own. "Standards are so high today," he said again and again. "But if something came along that I could fit myself into and contribute something to, I'd start working. I'm seventy and sometimes I feel every minute of it. When I have a good night's sleep, of course, I don't feel more than thirty or forty."

In April 1959, Irving and Ellin saw their second daughter, Linda Louise, marry a brokerage aide named Edouard Emmet. The service was at St. Thomas More Roman Catholic Church in New York City.

The Berlins were both happy at their daughter's happiness. But neither was happy about Irving himself. In his own words, he felt as if he were heading for a breakdown.

He wrote one song in 1959, called "Israel," a tribute to the state for which he had a great emotional attachment. The record industry, meanwhile, was happy to make hay with his old successes. One new album of old Berlin tunes followed upon the other. The Voice of America produced a two-hour show of tributes from people like Bing Crosby, Fred Astaire, Ginger Rogers, Eddie Cantor, Rudy Vallee, Ethel Merman, and many others who had worked with Berlin.

Ginger Rogers described him as "the apple pie sort of composer who makes you want to stand up and bleat out a song whether you can sing or not." Astaire said his old friend "dances mentally," and that was a great tribute to a man who could never step it much better than he could play it on a conventional piano. Cantor concentrated on Berlin the American. "He has always felt he'll never be able to repay the debt [he owes America] but he's never stopped trying."

All that leads up to a tribute which Berlin clearly prized above all others. President Eisenhower made a surprise appearance to say how much he admired the man who had been born in Siberia with the name Israel Baline.

"I can think of no one more deserving of today's tribute than Irving Berlin," said Ike. "He has contributed conscientiously of his time and talent in peace and in war to bring joy and entertainment to Americans everywhere. I venture that not one of us will ever forget the lovely and meaningful 'God Bless America.' "

In reply to this tribute, Berlin was straightforward. "I came here as an immigrant, and all the success I have I owe to my adopted country."

He had come to a new decision with the encouragement of Ellin and the family. He was ending the farce called retirement, the agony which was supposed to be a rest and which he couldn't fight.

"I'm not a kid anymore," he finally announced. "It takes a very rare person to retire gracefully, especially if he has been a success. My only hobby is songwriting." So he went back to work at the age of seventy-four.

21

Let's Take an Old-Fashioned Walk

"THE OLD MAN'S COMING back," they said at the Berlin Music Corporation. They said the same thing in Sardi's, and at the Algonquin, and *Variety* spread the story. Irving Berlin had come out of hibernation.

Berlin sent a note to the storage firm that had packed away some of his unneeded furniture and belongings. He wanted them to bring something up to his office on West Fifty-first Street.

When the storage men arrived, Berlin was as excited as a schoolboy. He had a room emptied out especially to receive the delivery, and when it was installed he stood back in pride. The Buick had come home again, an aging piece of oak with yellowed keys stained from holding lighted cigarettes.

Now he was determined to do his show about the retired general, to be called *Stars on My Shoulder*. He had been talking about it with the writing team of Howard Lindsay and Russell Crouse, who had done the book for *Call Me Madam*.

"Boys," he had said, "here's the idea I've got . . ."

The "boys" didn't like the idea all that much. Instead they asked, "How do you like the idea, Irving, of a musical based on a President who has just retired from office?"

Berlin liked the idea very much, mostly because the only thought he really had was that of going back into business. Looking back now, he says, "Their idea wasn't much, either." But what

Lindsay and Crouse had done was give new faith to a man who needed to be wanted again. Once more Berlin paced the floor instead of slouching at his easel or getting in the way at home.

Berlin was so grateful to be noticed again that he even granted interviews, though he didn't much like the angle that everyone was interested in his age. At least he was looking and feeling healthier than he had for years.

In Boston for the first tryout of *Mr. President*, for which Robert Ryan had the title role and Nanette Fabray played his wife ("doubling for Jackie Kennedy" was how *Time* magazine described the part), Berlin seemed to have more energy than all the rest of the cast put together.

"Whether you are twenty-four, sixty-four, or seventy-four," he told the show's team as he played over his score for them, "makes no difference. The only thing that counts is how good the show is." And he felt he had a good show. Reports of his enthusiasm had spread so that, once the stars had been signed, advance ticket orders began to pour in. Some two million dollars had been paid into the Broadway box office when *Mr. President* opened in Boston. Money still flooded in the day after the opening despite the opinions of the critics.

They gave Berlin even worse notices than he'd gotten for *Miss Liberty*.

Elliot Norton, in the *Boston Record*, said of the show, "Dreadful is the only word. Anything milder would be misleading, not to say dishonest. Never in his whole career has Irving Berlin written so many corny songs."

And reporting to its readers in London, the critic from the *Daily Herald* asked sadly, "Should he at seventy-four have stayed in retirement?" He went on, "Has America's Mister Music lost his magic touch? Certainly *Mr. President* has a bouncing fast-moving rhythm, gaily punctuated songs, some excellent catchy lyrics and punchy lines. But that legendary Berlin touch is obviously and oh so sadly missing."

Producer Leland Hayward, along with everyone else, read the

papers and felt sick. One writer said it "bogs down in tedium," another that it was in "dreadful shape."

"It's much as we felt ourselves," Hayward said, "but we're making changes. And don't forget, critics don't know anything about musicals."

And when the show opened in Washington for another pre-Broadway tryout, people were wishing it as well there as if they had heard nothing but glowing tributes. It was treated with glitter, as one of the finest shows the capital had ever known. President and Mrs. Kennedy were there. Everyone appeared to enjoy the evening immensely. It ended with a party given by Vice President Lyndon B. Johnson and Lady Bird.

"Has there ever been as dull a President as the man occupying the White House in *Mr. President?*" asked *The New York Times.* Although it said that Irving Berlin "gives the First Lady several lively songs, the book is patched together out of remnants of lame topical allusions, pallid political jokes, and stale gags based on White House tribal customs."

"Mr. Berlin," it went on, "missed on Broadway in recent years, is not at his best but his second best is superior to the generality of machine-made songs.

"There is typical Berlin sweetness in 'Pigtails and Freckles,' a romantic lilt in 'Don't Be Afraid of Romance' and rhythmic buoyancy in 'Laugh It Up' and 'Glad to Be Home Again.' "

Even if the show itself didn't have much life in it, the fact that a respected critic could still say a couple of his tunes had "rhythmic buoyancy" made Berlin feel "glad to be home again." It was all great therapy for him.

Time magazine, however, could hardly have been more cruel. It compared the show "with the maiden voyage of the S.S. *Titanic.* It left port with a glittering credits list; on board were Irving Berlin, Howard Lindsay, Russell Crouse, Leland Hayward, Joshua Logan.

"As it ploughed through the murky theatrical waters of Boston and Washington, iceberg-cool critics put sizeable holes in its hull.

Drifting into view on Broadway, *Mr. President* carried a trapped and talented crew that seemed to take comfort in huddling together at the finale to sing an Irving Berlin version of 'Nearer, My God to Thee' called 'This Is a Great Country.' But unlike the unsinkable *Titanic, Mr. President* will take at least two years to go under. It has more than $2,650,000 in advance ticket sales." *Time* went on, *"Mr. President* should have been rousingly rah-rah; instead, it is mostly nah-nah." The next week its "Time Listings" described it as "the worst musical on Broadway. But advance ticket sales will make it as durable as a bad penny."

It wasn't quite so durable, however. It closed after only a short run.

"I thought the show was going to run five years," Berlin told me. "But no one appeared interested in an ex-President." There was enough interest though, certainly enough sentiment, for a special "Tony" award to Berlin "for his distinguished contribution to the musical theater for these many years."

He wouldn't have been human not to feel that the award for the show was almost a "posthumous" one. Earlier he had said, "I don't think we have a Pulitzer Prize show, a Critics Circle Award show. I *do* think that we have a show that audiences will love. Of course, it would be nicer if the critics like us, too. And I wouldn't turn down a Pulitzer Prize or a Critics Award." But he had to content himself with the special Tony.

Not very long before, he would have been depressed about *Mr. President.* Now he was happier than he had been for a long time. His new songs hadn't been hits, but neither had a lot of the thousand or so tunes he had published over the previous half century.

Looking back at the show more than ten years later, Berlin frankly admitted that it was bad. "The critics said it was reminiscent. Of course it was. I had done it all before." Once more, the way Berlin looks at it, he was beaten by his own competition. "We all got off on the wrong foot. If you have a bad tune or a bad lyric, you can do something about it. But when you start off with a bad show or a bad book it's difficult to fix."

But being in trouble with *Mr. President* didn't worry him.

"Listen," he told Ellin, "I'd rather be 'unhappy' doing something than really being unhappy doing nothing."

When his seventy-fifth birthday came around in 1963, he and Ellin went off as usual to the Catskills together. "As you get older, it becomes a date," he said as he got into his car, still looking dapper in an English-made suit, still with plenty of black in his wavy hair.

"I feel as good as I've felt for a long time." And he had good reason to. The Screen Producers Guild had announced that he was going to be the winner of their eleventh annual Milestone Award for "historic contributions to movies." The Guild made the presentation at a special dinner for Irving and Ellin. He was greeted with the sort of genuine affection that's rare in Hollywood. Plenty of people who have been publicly worshipped there have been privately hated. No one ever felt that way about Irving Berlin. And so when Ginger Rogers, Rosalind Russell, Dinah Shore, and Yvette Mimieux joined Berlin around a piano that night, the thousand guests cheered as loudly as if they had each won an Oscar. Berlin was thrilled as he hadn't been for years. There was an almost visible lump in his throat when he played "God Bless America" and every one of the guests honoring him stood up.

There were two reasons for his being in Hollywood and they both meant what he needed most, the chance to work and the chance to be recognized.

He had signed a deal with MGM to make a super-spectacular musical that was finally, *really*, going to be called *Say It with Music*. And when he finished that, he was going to do another picture with Ethel Merman. He really felt as though he had "the sun in the morning and the moon at night." But it was the *Say It with Music* picture which excited him most.

Everyone but MGM and Berlin himself thought that the picture was going to be his life story—at last. As if to be certain that no one tried anything of the kind, Irving and Ellin took a house in Hollywood.

"I'm a man without a hobby," he said when he arrived. "They think I'm crazy to go on working. But if I rest, I get restless. So what is there to do but work? It isn't the money. I've plenty of that and it's coming in all the time from royalties. It's just that I'm not a tennis or golf man, I can't stand bridge and I'm too restless for chess."

There were rumors that Frank Sinatra was going to play in the MGM film. All Berlin knew at that early stage was that "my songs will serve as period identifications from 'Alexander's Ragtime Band' to 'Let's Have Another Cup of Coffee' and on past the Depression."

But something went wrong and MGM didn't get around to making the movie that year. It was rescheduled for 1964. Berlin was patient. When a young writer asked him for his philosophy of songwriting, he said: "You have to be patient and you have to have a heart. Too many songwriters today are mechanical. But if you write with a heart, you can't fail."

Irving Berlin may not be the easiest man to get to know (his friend and contemporary Irving Caesar, the man who wrote the lyrics for dozens of hits ranging from "Swanee" to "Tea for Two," chides him for "never being around with the boys") but once you have his friendship, you have earned yourself a loyalty for life.

There was the time, for instance, when Sam, the father of his friend Irving Hoffman, was due to celebrate his eighty-first birthday. Berlin decided there was only one present he wanted to give the old man. He wrote him a song called "Sam, Sam, the Man What Am."

Once the song was written, he hired a small group, booked a recording studio, and presented a record to the retired schoolmaster as "something from the other Irving." For all the Hoffman birthdays after that, Berlin updated the song (one year Mitch

Miller made a private recording of it) as a birthday present for Sam.

Berlin put off his concern over MGM's postponement. There were pressing family matters to involve him. The Berlins' youngest daughter, Elizabeth, was getting married. Irving gave the bride away in the London church of St. George's in Hanover Square. The bridegroom was publisher Edmund Fisher.

London newspapers were delighted by the visit. Herbert Kretzmer, in the *Daily Express*, was glad to see Berlin looking so "spruce, shaved and willing to talk" so early in the morning. In fact, he said he "beamed good will and benevolence in all directions."

He was a "happy and chatty man, giving the lie to the stories of extreme reticence that had preceded him." Berlin was in a good mood and nothing made him more exuberant than being adored by his public.

"I'm a ham. I think to be good at anything, you must like to show off what you do." Kretzmer said that Berlin's voice sounded "like an egg, softly cracked."

Berlin told him, "I've never been a smart alec. By the time I had sharpened the tools of my trade, I found that I wrote simple songs because that's how they came out of my head. I didn't try to change anything. A certain emotional something went into the songs and I never tried to analyze it too much. You can get *too* clever, you know."

Then it was back to Hollywood, to get *Say It with Music* underway again. Cecil Beaton, who had done the sets for *My Fair Lady*, was going to be called in for this. But Beaton wasn't called in, and again *Say It with Music* was postponed.

Why? Neither Berlin nor MGM could come up with a one-answer reason. Just when Berlin thought the whole deal was settled, it seemed that a combination of the rock 'n' roll era and the expense of running a giant Hollywood studio were having a negative effect. Of course, if Berlin agreed to having his life story filmed . . . But Berlin wanted no part of a deal like that.

Then suddenly he had legal problems of a different sort.

MAD magazine had printed a parody of "A Pretty Girl Is Like a Melody." And this one made his blood boil:

> Louella Schwartz
> Describes her malody
> To anyone in sight.
> She will complain
> Dramatize every pain.
> And then she'll wail
> How doctors fail
> To help her sleep at night.

The matter went to the United States Court of Appeals. Although Berlin's lawyer Simon Rifkind describe the MAD parody as "the worst kind of piracy. Piracy on the High C's," there wasn't much real levity on the songwriter's side of the fence.

In the court, the judge plainly sided with the magazine which, he said, had changed a song that "originally was a tribute to feminine beauty into a burlesque of a feminine hypochondriac."

Judge Irving R. Kaufman concluded finally that "parody and satire are deserving of substantial freedom both as entertainment and as a form of social and literary criticism." And as if to prick the conscience of the music business, he went on: "Through depression and boom, war and peace, Tin Pan Alley has light-heartedly insisted that the whole world laughs with a laugher and that the best things in life are free.

"But," he said, "in an apparent departure from these delightful sentiments," songwriters felt that MAD had "struck a sour note" in parodying their compositions. It was inevitable that MAD should use the same meter, if the original song were to be recognized through the effects of the parody. "We doubt that even so eminent a composer as Irving Berlin should be permitted to claim a property interest in iambic pentameter," said the judge.

So Irving Berlin ordered an appeal against this verdict. Six months later, in October 1964, the Supreme Court upheld the original judgment.

In January 1965, Berlin himself issued an edict to allow a change in one of his lyrics in the song that first made him a household name.

If anyone objected to singing a line like ". . . so nat-ural that you want to go to war," he agreed they could make it ". . . so nat-ural that you want to hear some more." Fifty-four years after first writing it, Irving Berlin was allowing a change in "Alexander's Ragtime Band."

He said he had "acknowledged a few objections to the spirit of the original line. You can't change something that's been established in the public mind. They don't take it literally. However, the alternative line is available for anyone who doesn't want to sing the original."

When his seventy-seventh birthday came around, he said, "The question is, 'Are you going to be a crabby old man or are you going to write another song?' "

Instead of being crabby, he produced seven new titles for *Say It with Music*, which MGM now said was going to be made after all, at a cost of four million dollars.

There were some lovely new titles, "One-Man Woman," "Whisper It," "Outside of Loving You, I Like You," even a nice social commentary on the times, "The Ten Best Undressed Women."

But the main attractions of *Say It with Music* were to be the twenty-five Berlin standards from the past, including the title tune. Movie-goers waited, and went on waiting.

By 1966, the project began to look permanently shelved. But people did hear a new Berlin song from the stage that year, and they loved it. At Lincoln Center in New York, those who crowded into the New York State Theater and heard his "An Old-Fashioned Wedding," weren't seeing a new show but a new edition of *Annie Get Your Gun*. Ethel Merman again played the title role. "She can play it till she's ninety," Berlin said, "and I hope she does."

Certainly Ethel has always had a soft spot for the show and "Old-Fashioned Wedding" was the best Berlin had done in years.

People were now calling him an "institution."

"I don't like that word," he said. "You know the old gag—who the hell wants to live with an institution? Let's use the word 'success.' I like that better. Some people think I work too hard but the important thing for me is to keep going."

And he told *The New York Times* in Toronto, as he got ready on his seventy-eighth birthday for a special six-week run of *Annie,* that his age wasn't a "specially notable achievement."

"People always make a big *tzimmis* about he's seventy-eight and still wants to keep working," he was fond of saying, slipping into the Yiddish in which he was still so much at home.

When he saw the way "Old-Fashioned Wedding" was selling, he was pleased to say, "Call it ego, if you like. But I'm very proud and very pleased to write a song at this point that's a hit."

Ellin and Irving now had a house on Beekman Place, near the East River. "I've always lived near this river, ever since I came to New York," he is fond of saying. "It's in a more swanky neighborhood maybe, but the same tugboats pass by."

What he desperately wanted to do in the late sixties was write a musical about that river. "I've got a few bits and pieces for it. A few songs. It's a big project. I may never do it."

What the papers said about "Old-Fashioned Wedding" gave Berlin incentive to try. The *New York World Journal Telegraph* said, "So welcome back Annie. Goodbye Dolly. Move over Mame. From now on, it's every girl for herself."

And the *New York Times* commented, "It's Tin Pan Alley all right but out of the top drawer."

Nor could he completely forget *Say It with Music.* The cost of the production had now escalated to between ten million and twelve million dollars, and Shirley MacLaine was said to be joining Sinatra to play the couple whose life was to be mirrored by Berlin's songs.

Betty Comden and Adolph Green had written a screenplay that everyone seemed to like and Berlin was now talking about the money he was going to make from it. "Not as much as I've gotten for other pictures," he said. "And much less than it's worth." He was deadly serious about that.

After all, "I get a lot of money in Hollywood because I've made money for them. Money makes the market. The best pictures are those that make money. They become artistic later."

In 1967, ASCAP issued a special publication in tribute to "a writer who has come a long and impressive way since his first song was published. He is talented, quick, versatile, modest, realistic, romantic, generous and committed to his craft." Finally, said the only trade union to which Berlin ever belonged, "he is the youngest and brightest old pro star in the firmament of American music."

People in the business went on talking about him, even if he wasn't around quite so much. When the team from *This Is the Army* had a reunion to mark the twenty-fifth anniversary of the show, Berlin sent a telegram of good wishes from the Catskills. He was, of course, the principal topic of conversation.

When he and Ellin went away for Christmas it was most often to Florida. "I like sunny Christmases," he confessed apologetically.

On May 10, 1968, Irving Berlin was eighty years old. To honor an occasion that had far more than just personal significance, American television gave him a special birthday party with Ed Sullivan as host.

It was a show that spanned the generations from Berlin himself to Diana Ross and The Supremes. And it was a tribute to Berlin as an American. Even President Lyndon B. Johnson took time off to tape a personal tribute to his favorite songwriter. "America is richer for his presence," said LBJ.

CBS brought on the biggest collection of stars in anyone's memory. Bing Crosby began at the beginning with "Marie from Sunny Italy," thus negating Berlin's boast that the song had never earned him more than thirty-seven cents in royalties. Robert Goulet sang one of Berlin's newest songs, "I Used to Play by Ear," and The Supremes gave their own sound to "Always" and "Say It with Music." Sullivan brought out a cake with eighty candles and Berlin came on to sing "God Bless America." Everyone said, "It was a schmaltzy but a wonderful party."

In New York's Central Park, 8,000 Girl Scouts—100 for every year of his age—said thanks for "God Bless America" and sang "Happy Birthday, dear Irving," as he drove into the park in an open car with Mayor John Lindsay.

What more could a man have asked? Except, of course, to go back a few years, write a few more shows, and eventually see *Say It with Music* come to the screen.

22

...And the Melody Lingers On

THE WORLD OF RAGTIME LONG ago gave way to swing which Berlin said would never last. It didn't. Jive came, and be-bop, and then rock 'n' roll took over.

Irving Berlin occasionally still sits by a one-key piano and gets an idea for a song. Then he calls in his musical secretary for notation and later hopes the song will get into the charts and demonstrate that the "mob" has improved its tastes.

Pounding the piano (he plays with all ten fingers, he points out, not just the two he's sometimes been accused of) is still doing wonders for Irving Berlin at the age of eighty-six. Hearing his tunes on stereo or television also lifts his spirit.

"My songs sound better than ever today," he says without feigning modesty. "And they pay more, too. Royalties and recording fees have gone up."

He is not so much a shy man as one who believes that his life is his own affair. Friends will talk about him avidly and then call to check with the "old man" to make sure that what they said was all right.

A musician who played jazz at the same time that Israel Baline was still serving beer told me, "I can't say anything. Izzy would sue me." Another checked with someone else who had been a close colleague and said, "I can't talk. When I telephoned I was

211

told, 'You know, you've always said you'd mind your own business.' "

Berlin will talk for hours on the telephone, the instrument he immortalized in his "All Alone." He is, of course, far from alone. His wife Ellin still adores him, as do his daughters and grandchildren. When he hears old friends like Bing Crosby or Fred Astaire on radio or television, he'll call them up the next day to tell them just how much he enjoyed their performances. Then he'll send them tapes of his own new songs and ask for opinions.

When he hears a disk jockey discussing pop music, he's likely to phone him, too, to tell him his own views. But he won't go on the air himself.

Nor will he bend to requests to pen his own memoirs, each one offering more money than the previous one. "I always give them the same answer, 'I can't write.' Maybe one day, after I'm gone, my wife will write my story. She knows me better than anyone else. But she won't do it while I'm still alive.

"I've told the same thing to many of my friends who want to write about me. This seems to be open season now for biographies, but I don't want anyone to write mine—yet."

And he *still* says no to any suggestions that at last this might be the time to make his filmed life story, whether or not they call it *Say It with Music.* "What the hell would I do with a handsome leading man impersonating me? I'm not handsome. Besides, if I were a studio head I wouldn't want to do the Irving Berlin Story with him breathing down my neck telling me how to do it."

He is conscious of the need to protect not only his own privacy but that of the family he loves. He has always done right by them—from the time he saved to buy Leah that rocking chair. He educated his daughters at Vassar, has seen them marry and have children. Today he has nine grandchildren "all of whom I love very much."

Which are Berlin's favorite songs? It depends on the mood he is in. Sometimes he is blunt and says the only ones he cares about are those that became hits. In that category he'll put "White

Christmas" at the head of the list because that has made him the most money. "But the one that is closest to me emotionally is 'God Bless America.' "

There are many who agree on the subject of "God Bless America." As recently as 1971, a minister, the Reverend Sue Sivking, petitioned that it be adopted as the American national anthem.

His chief complaint about the popular music scene today is just what it was in the thirties: not enough people make their own music now. "They don't sing songs so they don't get to know them."

He does concede that "there are some wonderful songs today." And he cites "The Impossible Dream" and "Little Green Apples" as examples of wonderful songs written by composers of the seventies.

"But I'll tell you something. They weren't written by professional songwriters. A professional songwriter would never have rhymed 'little green apples' with 'and it don't snow in Minneapolis.'

"Shall I tell you what I would have said? 'God didn't make little green apples and we don't pray in churches and chapels.' "

Over the years his writing styles have changed. He long ago abandoned rhyming 'n' with 'm.' Whereas he used to write tunes first and fit the words later, he changed to doing it the other way around, at least coming up with an idea or even a title first.

Berlin still keeps an active interest in the firm of the Irving Berlin Music Corporation, though he rarely goes to the offices on the Avenue of the Americas. If he has any one pet interest it is The Music Box Theater. While he has bought and sold plenty of real estate in his time, The Music Box is still half his. In September 1971, when the theater celebrated its fiftieth birthday, Berlin was there for the jubilee posing for pictures in front of the marquee that advertised its current attraction, the play *Sleuth*. But he turned down any idea of a celebration. "I'd worry too much about it," he explained.

At last he is able to do what was once impossible—paint. When he first dabbled at it, he signed his work "Izzy" or "Vincent." Now he takes it more seriously and proudly writes "Irving Berlin" in the right-hand corner, sometimes with a musical note.

One of his most recent works, a picture of a bird in top hat, white tie, and tails, he gave to Fred Astaire. "I don't know why I started painting a bird, but then when I put a top hat on it, it reminded me immediately of you," he told Astaire.

"And I value it very highly," Fred says. "As highly as the world has valued Irving's music."

Berlin likes to paint, although he doesn't think he does it particularly well. "As a painter, I'm a pretty good songwriter," he says.

"It's nice to hear compliments about the many standards that I've written over the years. But I can also hear that little bird chirp, 'So what have you done lately?' "

What Irving Berlin has done lately is just what he has done for nearly seventy years. Given a great many people a very great deal of pleasure, taught generations how to sing, and put together shows that will live in audience memory as long as their individual tunes.

"I've always thought of myself as a songwriter," he says. "Do you want big words like 'composer'? I won't be modest. But I'm a songwriter like dozens and dozens of others. And as long as I'm able, whether the songs are good or bad, I'll continue to write them because songwriting is not just a business with me. It's everything."

Songs

This index comprises only the Berlin songs that are mentioned in this book.

Index

219